Famous Flyers

Claire Chennault

Amelia Earhart

Charles Lindbergh

Eddie Rickenbacker

Manfred von Richthofen

Chuck Yeager

Famous Flyers

Eddie Rickenbacker

Rachel A. Koestler-Grack

CHELSEA HOUSE
PUBLISHERS

A Haights Cross Communications Company

Philadelphia

Frontis: Eddie Rickenbacker stands beside a plane bearing the "Hat in the Ring" insignia of the 94th Aero Squadron he commanded during World War I.

CHELSEA HOUSE PUBLISHERS

VP, NEW PRODUCT DEVELOPMENT Sally Cheney
DIRECTOR OF PRODUCTION Kim Shinners
CREATIVE MANAGER Takeshi Takahashi
MANUFACTURING MANAGER Diann Grasse

Staff for EDDIE RICKENBACKER

EXECUTIVE EDITOR Lee Marcott
ASSOCIATE EDITOR Bill Conn
PRODUCTION EDITOR Jaimie Winkler
PHOTO EDITOR Sarah Bloom
COVER AND SERIES DESIGNER Keith Trego
LAYOUT 21st Century Publishing and Communications, Inc.

A Haights Cross Communications ✦ Company

http://www.chelseahouse.com

First Printing

1 3 5 7 9 8 6 4 2

Library of Congress Cataloging-in-Publication Data

Koestler-Grack, Rachel A., 1973–
   Eddie Rickenbacker / Rachel Koestler-Grack.
      v. cm.—(Famous flyers)
Includes index.
Contents: The Atlanta crash—Boyhood—The working years—The racing years—
To the skies—Buying an airline—Lost in the Pacific—The later years.
   ISBN 0-7910-7215-0
   1. Rickenbacker, Eddie, 1890-1973—Juvenile literature. 2. Air pilots—United
States—Biography—Juvenile literature. 3. Air pilots, Military—United States—
Biography—Juvenile literature. 4. World War, 1914-1918—Aerial operations,
American—Juvenile literature. 5. World War, 1939-1945—Aerial operations,
American—Juvenile literature. [1. Rickenbacker, Eddie, 1890–1973. 2. Air pilots,
Military.] I. Title. II. Series.
TL540.R53 K64 2002
629.13'092—dc21

                                                    2002151350

CONTENTS

The Atlanta Crash

Lying in the twisted wreckage, Eddie tried to shake his mind free from shock. The plane had crashed. He was alive. Eddie decided to concentrate on staying that way. Cold rain was gently falling on what seemed to be never-ending blackness. Eddie was wedged tight in the wreck, his head pinned between the bulkhead and the gas tank and his left arm stuck under debris, crushing a nerve in his elbow. His entire left arm was paralyzed, but the crushed nerve was sending an excruciating pain to his left hand. The rain did not add much discomfort since he was already soaked in blood and high-octane gasoline. Around him Eddie heard voices and moans. He was not the only passenger alive.

From somewhere in the dark, Eddie heard a man's voice say, "Hey, let's start a bonfire and get warm."

"No!" Eddie yelled. "You'll set the gasoline on fire. For God's sake, don't light a match!" Panic pushed the words out of him, even though it hurt his chest to shout. Eddie later learned that some ribs had been broken, several in two or three places, and two pieces of broken bone had poked out his side.

"Who is that?" someone asked.

"Rickenbacker," Eddie replied. "Don't light a match. Just sit tight and wait. Somebody will come and get us."

It seemed ironic that after all the flying Eddie had done in World War I, dodging Boches and dancing with death, the American Ace of Aces was downed in a routine flight on his way

After surviving a plane crash in Atlanta that killed eight people and hospitalized him for four months in 1941, Eddie arrived in New York City triumphant and ready to resume his duties as president and general manager of Eastern Air Lines.

to a business meeting. But Eddie had escaped death by narrow margins many times before, and this time, he firmly believed, would be no different.

He replayed the flight from New York to Atlanta in his mind. On Wednesday, February 26, Eddie Rickenbacker boarded Eastern Air Lines Flight 21, scheduled to depart at 7:10 that night. He was en route to an important meeting with the directors of Eastern Air Lines in Miami on Friday. As president and owner of the company, it was imperative that Eddie attend. But before arriving in Florida, he planned to stop in Birmingham, Alabama, get a few hours' sleep, and attend a luncheon with the Birmingham Aviation Committee. After lunch, Eddie would take the afternoon plane to Atlanta and proceed to Miami that night.

Eddie sat in the "sky lounge" of the Mexico Flyer, a DC-3 sleeper equipped with berths. The sky lounge was a private room directly behind the cockpit. Eddie relaxed in his berth as he fingered through his paperwork. Over Spartanburg, South Carolina, the pilot entered the room and informed Eddie that the weather in Atlanta was not too good. They could have some difficulty landing. Having "the boss" on board probably heightened the pilot's apprehensiveness. Eddie simply told the captain to do what he felt was best, that he was in command. This response was Eddie's normal procedure. The plane continued to Atlanta.

The flight proceeded smoothly for a time after their conversation. Eddie saw the familiar lights of the Atlanta Federal Penitentiary through the scattered clouds as the plane flew over the city. They made an instrument approach. In this procedure, the plane followed the radio beam in over the airport, flew past it into a 180-degree turn, and came back on the radio beam. Eddie had taken this flight many cloudy nights, and everything seemed to be normal. The passengers had no way of knowing the plane was coming in 1,000 feet too low. Apparently, the pilot was not aware of this error either. Possibly the field gave the pilot the wrong altitude upon approach or the copilot misunderstood the readings.

Eddie felt the left wing go down into the 180-degree turn. Suddenly, the left wing scraped treetops. The pilot must have felt it, because he immediately pulled the left wing up and put the right wing down. Eddie jumped out of his seat and ran down the aisle toward the back of the plane. He could feel the pilot losing control. The right wing hooked the trees and ripped off, flipping the plane on its nose.

The plane went black as the pilot cut the ignition switch. Eddie was thrown around inside the somersaulting plane. His left hip came down hard on the arm of a seat, shattering it. The plane then landed on its tail and split in two, right down the middle. When the sound of twisting and tearing metal stopped, Eddie found himself right at the torn opening, pinned tight in the tangled wreckage. His left knee was broken. The only part of Eddie's body that had any movement whatsoever was his right hand and forearm.

He was lucky to be alive, but being confined in the wreckage was frustrating for him. He wanted to pull himself loose. He yanked his head with all his might, moving it just enough to make contact with a sharp piece of metal that was sticking out about three inches away from his left eye. The jagged edge sliced Eddie's eyelid in the center, and his eyeball popped out of its socket and landed on his cheek. Despite this, Eddie tried to wriggle his shoulders loose. In so doing, he snapped several ribs. He could hear them break and later described the sound as like that of popcorn popping. Not far from Eddie, two more passengers lay trapped in the wreck. From their moans of pain, Eddie could tell their condition was more severe than his. He tried to comfort them and assure them that help was on the way. But the words were not enough to save them, and they passed away waiting for the rescue crews.

During the night, one rescue party passed by the crash area. Eddie could hear their soft voices, but they were quite a distance away. He cried out to them, the effort sending sharp pains around his ribs, but it wasn't loud enough; they did not hear him or locate the plane. As frustrating as it was at the time, it was a good thing they kept on walking after all: Eddie believed that the search party's kerosene lamps would have sent them all up in flames. Finally, in the cold, gray light of dawn, the nine living passengers were finally discovered by another search party and rushed by ambulance to Piedmont Hospital in Atlanta.

Only two interns were on duty at the hospital that early in the morning. Eddie figured with his eye hanging out and his mangled body, he must have looked a horrible mess. The intern looked him over and told the attendants, "He's more dead than alive. Let's take care of the live ones." And they pushed him to the side.

Eddie was lying on a stretcher helpless and speechless when a Catholic priest entered the room. He asked the attendant what Eddie's religion was. If Eddie was Catholic, he would read him his last rites. Knowing he wasn't dead yet, and that he had no intention of dying, Eddie answered: "I'm a damn Protestant just like 90 percent of the people."

The answer was short and pointed, but it got results. The lead surgeon, Floyd W. McRae, immediately went to work on Eddie—his first order of business being to secure Eddie's eyeball back in its socket. The doctors then discussed how they were going to attempt to fix the rest of Eddie's injuries. After trying to manually align him with no success, and even managing to break a few more bones, they decided not to operate. Instead, they put him in a plaster cast that encased his entire body from his chin to his toes. The only cast-free part of his body was his right arm.

Eddie's wife, Adelaide, and his two sons, David and Bill, stayed at Eddie's bedside day and night until he seemed to show notable improvement. The boys left the Sunday morning following the crash to return to school, but Adelaide stayed with Eddie. Two hours after they left, Eddie took a turn for the worse. Eddie later wrote, "I felt the presence of death. I knew that I was going."

Adelaide called the state police and asked them to stop the bus on which the boys were traveling and bring them back. The patrol car picked them up and raced back at 80 to 90 miles per hour. David and Bill later admitted that they loved the exciting ride. The state troopers had to stop for gas along the way and told the station attendant to hurry because they were trying to get Eddie Rickenbacker's boys to his hospital bedside. The attendant told them that they didn't need to hurry anymore, that he had heard over the radio that Rickenbacker had died an hour ago. The troops brought the boys anyway, and they found out that the news report was wrong. Eddie was still alive, putting up a miraculous fight for his life.

For ten days, Eddie had to make a conscious effort to live. Death patiently sat beside him, and Eddie admitted that it would have been easy to die, but something inside of him told him he had to live. Slowly Eddie improved. Four months and two days after the crash, Eddie was released from Piedmont.

Eddie returned to New York with his family. He then bought a cottage on Candlewood Lake in Connecticut, which allowed him to spend three days a week in town and the other four with his family at Candlewood. During the summer and into the fall, as painful as it was, Eddie continued physical therapy. He hoped to return to work in the fall, but that goal proved to be too ambitious; he was still suffering a lot of pain.

Meanwhile, the United States went to war. Eddie and his wife were in New York on December 7, 1941. That morning, Eddie went down to his office, as he usually did, to write letters. News came over the radio that the Japanese had attacked Pearl Harbor. Immediately, Eddie returned home, where he and Adelaide followed the news the rest of the day and through the night. This was all the more incentive for Eddie to get fit again, and he spent days exercising and stretching his muscles, gradually becoming more limber.

Eddie and his wife, Adelaide, are shown here shortly before their wedding on September 16, 1922. Eddie had survived the perils of World War I, and his bravery and expertise would be called upon again during World War II over 40 years later.

One day in March, Eddie received a call from General H. A. "Hap" Arnold, the commanding general of the U.S. Army Air Force. He asked Eddie how his health was holding up. By then, Eddie had made a nice recovery, save a few scars and a permanent limp in his left leg, and he assured the general of such. General Arnold then informed Eddie that he had an important mission for him, but he couldn't relay it over the phone. He wondered if Eddie could come to Washington.

Eddie told the general he would be there the following Monday morning. He had no idea what mission was in store for him, but he knew it would involve the air force and, more important, the fight for freedom. In the hospital, Eddie had believed he was meant to live, and now he felt that this could be the purpose he was to serve. Eddie later wrote, "War is hell, but sometimes a necessary hell. When it comes, everyone should be proud to give his services unflinchingly to his country."

Boyhood

Edward Vernon Reichenbacher was born in the midwestern town of Columbus, Ohio, on October 8, 1890, to William and Elizabeth Basler Reichenbacher. (The spelling of Eddie's last name was changed during World War I; this book uses that chosen spelling— Rickenbacker—throughout.) His parents were natives of Switzerland who met in Columbus, fell in love, and were married. Elizabeth was a fair-skinned redhead of French descent who loved art and poetry. William was a tall, husky German with a thick mustache. He was stern and hardworking, and spent his first years in the United States as a railroad laborer.

Edward's parents saved their money to buy a 150-by-200-foot plot of farmland on the eastern side of Columbus. William built their house with his own hands and some credit. With no electricity or running water, the Rickenbacker house was simple and raw. To a young immigrant family, however, it was a piece of American heaven.

The day in 1893 that the East Livingston Avenue horsecar stopped at the end of the line and the Rickenbackers stepped off at their new home, the family was filled with pride and a sense of accomplishment. Edward was only three years old at the time, but the moment was filled with such excitement that it constituted one of his earliest, most impressionable memories. To his parents, this day was the end of a dream and the beginning of a wonderful reality.

When the Rickenbackers moved into their new home, Edward, called Eddie, was one of four children. His sister, Mary,

Eddie was born in Columbus, Ohio on October 8, 1890, where his immigrant parents worked hard to provide for the Rickenbacker family. Eddie learned the value of a strong work ethic, and adopted it in his own life.

was the oldest. Next was Eddie's older brother, William. Eddie was the third child, but followed closely in William's footsteps in an effort to be as big as and even braver than his older brother. The fourth child was Emma.

Four other children were born in the house on East Livingston. Louise died in infancy. Louis was a frolicking, fun-loving boy, followed by his opposite, serious and industrious brother, Dewey. The youngest member of the family was little Albert.

The Rickenbacker children learned to work together as well as play together. William and Elizabeth were loving parents but strict. They taught their children the traditional values of the Old World and that hard work was important. Eddie helped his mother plant cabbage, potatoes, and other vegetables. The Rickenbackers raised their own chickens, kept goats for milk, and from time to time fattened and butchered a pig.

As the Rickenbacker homestead grew and prospered, so did their patriotism. Eddie's parents believed that America was a wonderful place, where opportunities existed for every family. Eddie remembered his parents asking, "Where else could a man begin with nothing and feed his children apple pie for dessert?" This sense of pride as a countryman led his father to volunteer to fight with the U.S. Army in the Spanish-American War (1898–1902). When he arrived at the recruiting station, however, he learned that the war situation was not so severe that family men were required to sign up for the army. Although William did not actually fight for his country, the gesture made an impression on young Eddie. The love his parents had fostered for their adopted land, the land of Eddie's birth, moved Eddie to believe that there was something extraordinary about this country. He learned to love America.

In his childhood, Eddie proved to be of a mischievous nature. Some of his rebellious behavior was a result of the resentment he felt toward his brother's seniority. Bill was four years older and possessed a stronger physical build than Eddie. Bound and determined to earn respect above his age, Eddie

Recruiters in cities across the nation urged young men to volunteer for the Spanish–American War. William Rickenbacker's patriotism drove him to volunteer, but recruiters turned away men with families. However, Eddie was impressed by his father's willingness to give back to his country.

followed Bill around, imitating his every action. On one occasion, Eddie hid in a tree and watched Bill and his friends roll corn-silk cigarettes. As soon as the boys began puffing on their smokes, Eddie saw his opportunity to become one of the big boys via a good, old-fashioned, proven technique—blackmail. "Hey," he hollered, "I can see what you're doing. If you don't give me a smoke I'll snitch on you."

As more families moved into the neighborhood, Eddie found other boys struggling with big-brother problems. The boys formed a club they named the Horsehead Gang, a name derived from a sign that hung over a nearby racetrack entrance. The Horsehead Gang was the beginning of real trouble for Eddie. Some of their "games" spanned beyond mischievous and spilled into punishable, criminal behavior. One night, the crew sneaked out and broke the globes on the gas-burning streetlights on Miller Avenue. Before long, the police had the criminals pegged, and a policeman showed up at the Rickenbackers' door. After Eddie's father and the police officer had a chat about the Horsehead Gang, Eddie got his punishment—an Old World-style whipping.

Eddie continued to have temporary lapses into rebellious and reckless behavior. One such adventure took place when he was eight years old. The gang decided to take a "roller-coaster" ride on a steel cart into a gravel pit near Eddie's neighborhood. The pit was a deep quarry where, during the week, rock and gravel were hauled out by a cable that pulled the filled cart on rails. At noon every Saturday, the pit closed down. Eddie and his friends showed up there one Saturday afternoon and pushed the cart up the hundred-foot incline out of the pit. They kept it secured in place with wooden blocks as they climbed inside.

"Here goes nothing!" Eddie yelled and kicked the blocks from under the wheels and jumped inside. The cart rocked unsteadily as it gained speed rolling down the incline. Jerking and creaking, the cart sped out of control. In an instant, the cart flipped, throwing the other boys clear, but Eddie fell short. The cart ran right over the top of Eddie's leg and tumbled to the bottom of the pit. The laceration laid Eddie's leg open to the bone. This incident was one of Eddie's first brushes with near-death.

Then, at age nine, Eddie had a terrifying revelation: one day he would die and the world would move on without him. Eddie imagined the endless stretching of time, and a world that continued to change and grow in his absence. The thought was too agonizing for him to handle. He obsessed about the horrifying realization, and from time to time he would steal away into the barn alone. Collapsing into the straw, he would sob uncontrollably.

At one of these times, his father happened to find Eddie face down in tears. "What's the matter, Eddie?" he asked. Eddie tried to find the words to explain the painful realization he had come to.

Afterward, William chose a fitting solution to Eddie's problem: he grabbed a switch and gave Eddie a whack. "You're too young to think of things like that," he told Eddie. "Life and death are my worry, not yours. Don't ever let me catch you crying about such foolish things again."

Although the whipping did not banish Eddie's deep feelings of loss for the world he would not live to see, it did teach him that he shouldn't waste time brooding over the inevitable. Eddie decided to live life to the fullest as long as the good Lord gave him breath. After this epiphany, Eddie gave up his escapades with the Horsehead Gang and set out to find a more meaningful side of life.

Throughout Eddie's reckless and mischievous behavior, he never lost his faith in God. Elizabeth had carved the impressions of religion in the Rickenbacker children. Each night after supper, she would read passages from the Bible she had brought to America from Switzerland. Eddie sat with the other children as his mother opened the cover embossed in gold with the words "Heilige Bibel." Elizabeth often read the Sermon on the

Eddie Rickenbacker— the Artist

As a boy, Eddie tried to taste every dish on the buffet of possibility. For a while, he took up watercolor. He painted pictures of flowers, landscapes, and animals. One of his best still-life paintings he presented to his mother. For his father, he painted several Swiss landscapes, created from William's word descriptions. Next, Eddie moved on to music as a means of expression. For a few pennies, he purchased a nicked and bruised violin from a secondhand shop. With sanding and varnishing, however, the violin's finish shined so richly it seemed any sound that came from it would be beautiful. Eddie learned to play a few songs, but the interest did not take hold. Eddie was looking for a task that stretched beyond his home, his neighborhood, even his world. This desire eventually rooted itself in the world of business.

Mount and the twenty-third Psalm, stopping to discuss the meanings of the passages as she read and explaining how they applied to everyday life.

Elizabeth taught Eddie how to pray. Above all, she told him that the Lord was a friendly God, sympathetic to the problems of his children. Eddie carried this awareness of God through his life, addressing the Lord with respect, confident he would be listened to and answered.

Eddie believed that what constituted a man was a sense of duty, and until he found his responsibility and sense of purpose, he would still be just a boy. At age 10, Eddie found the "duty" he was looking for—a job delivering newspapers for the *Dispatch*. As insignificant as this small job may seem, to Eddie it was as important as any other job he might have. This job was his initiation into manhood. He got up at two o'clock in the morning, walked two miles to the *Dispatch* to pick up his papers, and then set out on his delivery route. As a newspaper boy, Eddie earned the steady income of a dollar a week.

In time, Eddie began to wonder if he could do better. He learned of a job picking strawberries for a penny a pint. This sounded like a more profitable enterprise, so he quit his work at the newspaper and began his employment as a strawberry picker. The strawberries Eddie picked were not as plump as the strawberries in today's supermarkets, and it took quite a few to fill a pint. But Eddie's speculations were correct—strawberry picking paid better than delivering newspapers.

Even with his work of becoming a responsible man, Eddie still had time for hobbies and games. In 1899, Eddie saw his first horseless carriage at the circus. It was a Duryea, a three-cylinder automobile designed by Charles Duryea. This sight led Eddie and his friends to build their own push-mobiles by mounting wooden wheels to long, flat boards. For axles, they used old water pipes greased with lard stolen from their mothers' kitchens. These early creations sparked Eddie's interest in the world of mechanics.

Eddie's passion for automobiles and the world of mechanics was sparked in 1899 when he first saw the Duryea. This 750-pound "horseless carriage" had a four stroke, four horsepower engine.

It was only natural that the next step would be to race these new "cars." The boys formed two-man teams for each push-mobile—a driver and a pusher. They would race around a homemade track, bumping and pushing, vying for the front position. At times, the race would end in a free-for-all, but no one was ever seriously injured. Eddie's push-mobiles were the first of their kind. He later told Chevrolet about them and his stories inspired the famous Soap Box Derby.

Around the same time, Roy Knabenshue, who was touring the country with a dirigible, made an appearance in Columbus. Everybody in town turned out to watch Knabenshue float above them in his airship. Eddie was particularly captivated by this amazing phenomenon. He too wanted to fly like Roy Knabenshue and went to work thinking up a way.

At last he came up with an idea. He bought a large, farm-wagon umbrella at a second-hand store and attached it to his bicycle. His plan was to ride the bicycle off the slanted roof of a nearby barn. He figured that, with the speed and height, the umbrella would lift him over the ground like a bird.

But Eddie was not about to test his theory without allow-ing for the possibility of failure. For a few days prior to liftoff, he hauled carts of sand to a spot beside the barn, figuring that the pile of sand would help provide a soft break in case of a crash. When he felt the sand pile was high enough, he commis-sioned his close friend Sam Wareham as his personal assistant and the two of them pulled the bike to the roof peak. Sam steadied the bike while Eddie climbed on. The ground was a long way down, but the thought of flying like Roy Knabenshue was enough to override Eddie's fear.

"Okay, Sam," Eddie said. "Let go!"

The bicycle gained momentum as Eddie rode it down the steep roof. When it left the roof's edge, something occurred that Eddie had not planned for. The speed and resistance caused by the air made the umbrella turn inside out. With a loud pop, Eddie lost all hope of flight. Down he went into the sandpile. Luckily, he was momentarily stunned but unscathed. The bicycle, however, suffered greater injury; it was totaled. That was the end of Eddie Rickenbacker's first flight, but little did he know that in the future he'd have his share of air time.

In Eddie's youth, he experienced several other brushes with death aside from his quarry ride with the Horseheads and his attempted flight on the bicycle flying machine. One such instance occurred during the winter of his first year at school. While he was attending East Main Street public school in Columbus, a fire started in the school basement and quickly spread. The fire bell rang out, and the teachers shuffled the children out to safety,

Eddie included. Before long, the fire wagons arrived, pulled by horses, and Eddie was taken in by the excitement of the men fighting the fire. Then suddenly, a horrifying thought crossed Eddie's mind. In all the rush and confusion, he had left his hat and overcoat hanging inside the burning school. All Eddie could concentrate on was the fury he would have to endure from his mother if he came home without his coat and cap.

Without a second thought, Eddie tore away from the other children and ran straight into the schoolhouse. As he jumped through the flames that blocked his classroom door, he could feel their intense heat hitting his face. He heard the hissing of his eyebrows and hair as they were singed by the fire. He ran into the coatroom, grabbed his belongings, and dashed back through the wall of flame.

As he exited the building, Eddie realized what he had just done and how badly he could have been hurt. He reached the other children and continued running. Without stopping once, he ran a mile and a half to his home and straight into his mother's arms, still grasping his coat and hat.

By the time Eddie was 13 years old, the Rickenbacker family had increased their number of chickens and goats and added two rooms onto the house. His siblings Mary and Bill both held jobs and contributed to the family's income. The family was by no means rich, but it was outside of the clutches of discomfort.

Over the years, William refined his skills in construction and became a foreman and equipment operator for a local company, building bridges throughout central Ohio. William often took Eddie to the construction sites. As the two would look out at the bridgework over Alum Creek or Big Walnut River, William would explain to Eddie the meaning of his work. He would tell Eddie stories about the early pioneers, crossing the river by ox and wagon. William then told Eddie how these bridges would allow more people to travel and travel quickly, bringing this big country closer together.

Eddie watched the anticipation sparkle in his father's eyes as he spoke in his German accent, "Soon it will be finished. . . . And mark my words, Eddie. You're going to see more and more of them."

One evening when William was working a pile driver on the night shift, he stopped in the workshop before leaving to see what Eddie was doing. Eddie was busy building a perpetual motion machine that he was sure would bring him fame and fortune. But the way in which Eddie was building it would never make it run, and William saw this flaw. He asked Eddie what the machine's purpose was. As Eddie searched for a response, William continued to explain that a machine is no good without a purpose.

After William made this comment, he asked Eddie to remember two things. He told him not to get involved with a machine that he did not know how to control. Secondly, he repeated that there was no value in a machine that would not serve a useful purpose. Then William talked about a couple of brothers who were working on a flying machine. Many people thought the Wright brothers were out of their minds. But William valued their imagination and saw the wonderful purpose of a flying machine.

"Eddie," he said, "you're a lucky boy to be born when you were. There are a lot of new things in the making, and you ought to be ready to have a hand in them."

Those words were the last Eddie heard from his father. That night, while William worked the pile driver, he was struck in the head by a swinging timber. The impact fractured his skull, leaving him comatose for several days. He gained consciousness and recognized his family just before he passed away on August 26, 1904.

The body was brought to the house on East Livingston, and relatives and friends stopped by to pay their last respects. Elizabeth asked the children to take one last look at their father. She then asked them to be sure to remember each other as they grew up and moved away, and to promise that if one became more successful than the others, he or she would help the others with their needs.

The night after the body was buried in the cemetery, Eddie woke to a noise downstairs. He found his mother crying at the kitchen table with her head in her hands. Wanting to find words to comfort her, he told her that he would never make her cry again. Elizabeth gave Eddie a pat on the head. He pulled a chair up beside her, and the two sat together silently. It took a while for Eddie to realize that he was sitting at the head of the table, in the chair in which his father had always sat. In the years following, Eddie would come to understand his new place in his family's home.

The Working Years

Although Eddie felt the burden of financial responsibility to his family, to the rest of the world he was an underdeveloped 13-year-old kid. Eddie wondered where he would get a job and whether his mother would let him take a job if he could find one. In these desperate times, Eddie felt it best to get a job first and ask permission later.

Eddie knew finding an employer to hire him would not be easy. He was still in the seventh grade. According to labor laws, a boy had to be 14 years old and through the eighth grade before he could legally work. In addition, he could not rely on his brother Bill to pull a few strings, because Bill would tell his mother.

After much thought, Eddie remembered that Bill had once worked for the Federal Glass Factory. If the factory had employed one Rickenbacker, there was a good chance they would hire another. The next morning, Eddie got ready for school as usual and started out with the other children. As soon as he was out of the sight of the house, Eddie turned his steps toward the glass factory. He walked into the factory employment office and introduced himself as Eddie Rickenbacker, Bill's brother. Eddie informed them he was looking for a job, and to avoid any uncomfortable questioning, he added that he was fourteen and had finished the eighth grade.

The workers looked at him, not altogether convinced he was telling them the truth. But Eddie's determination must have won them over. He was told to report to work at six o'clock

When he was only 13 years old, Eddie worked the night shift at a glass factory. The hours were long and the work was grueling, but Eddie felt a responsibility to lessen his family's financial burden.

that evening. He would work from six at night until six in the morning—twelve hours—and if he couldn't handle it, they added, he shouldn't bother showing up.

"I'll be here," Eddie assured them.

Eddie nearly ran the entire two miles back home. He had gotten a job. Elizabeth did not share her son's excitement. She wanted him to finish his studies. Before she had time to put up much of an argument, Eddie was pleading with her to let him take the job. As he pleaded, her eyes filled with tears. So, even though Eddie had promised her he'd never make her cry, already that promise was being broken. But Elizabeth finally gave in to Eddie's begging. With William's income gone, she didn't have much choice. At 4:30 the next evening, with a lunch pail in hand, Eddie started out for the Federal Glass Factory.

At the factory, Eddie watched the skilled glassblowers fashion glass tumblers one at a time. Eddie then carried them on a heavy steel platter to the tempering ovens. The workers took a short break at midnight; Eddie had just enough time to finish his sandwich and then was back to work.

Night after night of hard work took a heavy toll on Eddie. But at the end of the week, he was handed a small brown envelope that lessened the soreness in his muscles. Inside were three dollar bills and a silver half-dollar coin—his first payday. When he got home, he handed the envelope to his mother and watched her eyes brighten as she looked inside. Eddie felt the pride of the moment well in his chest.

In the beginning, Eddie's foreman at the factory, John Crawford, scared him with his rough and hard talk. Before long, however, Eddie discovered a compassionate side of the man. Crawford appreciated Eddie's enthusiasm, and gave him more responsibilities as the weeks progressed. He even allowed Eddie to take short naps behind the ovens from time to time. When he discovered Eddie asleep, he'd give him a kick and threaten to fire him. But he always let him sleep a while longer.

The other workers also took a liking to Eddie. During the midnight break, they taught him how to make flowers out of colored glass. The blowing required to make these delicate pieces took quite a bit of lung power, but the way Elizabeth's eyes softened when Eddie presented her with his creations made all the puffing worthwhile.

With the long night hours, Eddie felt himself becoming more and more run down. During the afternoon, he still had chores to do at home. That, on top the hard factory work, was about enough to do him in. One night, he walked into Mr. Crawford's office and told him he was quitting. Mr. Crawford seemed surprised. "Don't you like it here?" he asked. Eddie simply replied that he didn't like working at night. At three o'clock in the morning, he walked out of the Federal Glass Company, an unemployed 13-year-old. The thought never occurred to him that he may not be able to find another job. He was an energetic youth, willing to do work, and he had complete confidence in his own determination.

Early the next morning, Eddie went to the Buckeye Steel Casting Company. He was first in line when the employment office opened. Just as he had at the glass company, Eddie told the man at the desk that he was 14 years old and had experience in making molds and castings. The man told him to report to work at seven o'clock.

Eddie soon found out that making cores for steel castings was hard and messy work. However, at his new job, Eddie worked an hour less, from seven in the morning to six in the evening, and he was working during the day. And, although at the time of his job acceptance, Eddie had neglected to ask what his starting pay would be, when the weekend came, Eddie learned he was earning a dollar a day—six whole dollars a week. With money like that, Eddie felt the Rickenbacker family would soon be clear of financial stress.

With his upgraded responsibilities, Eddie was soon supervising his younger siblings in house chores. The daytime work schedule gave Eddie some free time in the evening, so he took a second job setting up pins at a newly opened bowling alley for five cents a game. On Saturday and Sunday nights, Eddie sometimes brought home over 50 cents. In addition to furnishing his family with income, Eddie began tidying up the yard, planting grass, and adding a picket fence.

In his new life as a working man, Eddie lost touch with his neighborhood friends. His days with the Horsehead Gang became a memory. For relaxation, he would sometimes take a streetcar ride to Olentangy Park on Sunday afternoons. There, he would ride the merry-go-round or the Ferris wheel for a nickel. Some Sundays he bought a box of Cracker Jacks. At the end of his leisurely afternoon, he would take the streetcar back home, enjoying the peace of the Sunday evening streets.

Eddie held a couple of other jobs after his time at the steel factory, including one at a shoe factory and another at a stone monument manufacturing company. Each employer was as equally impressed as the last with Eddie's hard work and dedication. But Eddie was always searching for the most interesting and challenging work he could find. He sometimes quit a job with higher pay to take lower-paying work with a new employer from whom he believed he could learn more.

One afternoon while strolling the streets of Columbus, Eddie noticed a crowd gathering on the corner of High and Broad Streets. Eddie's curiosity was piqued and he hurried over to see what was causing the commotion. There in the street Eddie saw the most beautiful sight of his young life—a brand new Ford turtleback roadster, the first in Columbus. The car's owner gave an informal lecture about his new treasure, detailing the automobile's performance and adding that one day, every person would own one.

Caught up in the excitement of the moment, Eddie spoke out: "Mister, do you ever take anybody for a ride?"

The crowd quieted as the man looked Eddie up and down. "Why?" he asked.

As usual, Eddie kept his confident nature at the surface, and pushed any fear of forwardness deep inside himself. "Well," he answered, "I'd like to take a ride."

To Eddie, the seconds before the man's response seemed to tick by slower than the nights at the glass factory. But finally the man nodded and told Eddie to hop in. That ride around the block was one of the biggest moments in Eddie's life. As they cruised along at ten miles an hour, Eddie held on tight. This was the swiftest ride he'd ever taken. He felt the pride of tremendous opportunity. Eddie became an instant admirer of the automobile, a passion that would take him to a new level in his career life.

Even at 15 years old, Eddie could see the future of the automobile. He believed that before long, these machines would be crawling through every town and dotting the countryside. Excited and ambitious, Eddie wanted desperately to be a part of this industry. This desire led Eddie to Evan's Garage on Chestnut Street. Evan's advertised automotive repairs and storage. Eddie began working as a shop boy at the garage for seventy-five cents a day, a considerable pay cut from his previous jobs. But Eddie didn't mind. In his opinion, it was not a step back, but chance at a unique opportunity. Eddie capitalized on his good fortune, and took every free moment to learn about these incredible machines.

In 1905, the internal combustion engine was still in development. Therefore, many horseless carriages were powered by electric batteries. Electric power provided a smooth and simple acceleration, but the batteries were in constant need of charging. This function was key to the business of Evan's Garage, which both charged and built automobile batteries. With Eddie in the shop, the managers could solicit business while Eddie charged batteries and kept the shop running. When they were out of the shop, Eddie would be

These electric cars are recharging at a substation much like Evan's Garage, where Eddie worked recharging car batteries. Eddie took a pay cut to work at the garage, but considered the position an opportunity to learn more about his passion—cars.

sitting in the cars, pretending. He would drive them forward and back in the garage.

After working at Evan's Garage for six months, repairing cars and charging batteries ceased to satisfy Eddie's growing ambitions. He wanted to learn more. He wrote letters to numerous colleges in an attempt to find a correspondence course in automotive engineering. After several negative responses, Eddie discovered the International Correspondence School (ICS) in Scranton, Pennsylvania. ICS taught a complete course in mechanical engineering, including a special section on automobiles and internal combustion engines. This course was just what Eddie was searching for.

Also, only two blocks from Evan's Garage, the Frayer-Miller Company was making actual automobiles, right in Columbus. The factory turned out about one car a month. With Eddie's interests expanding, he wanted to find a way to get inside that company. He began hanging around the plant on Sunday mornings, just to watch the workers. He noticed that in addition to a stock touring car, the factory was building three racing cars. The cars were to be entered in the Vanderbilt Cup Race. The thought of racing cars set Eddie on fire.

Lee Frayer was the designer and chief engineer of both the engines and the cars. He appeared to Eddie to be hardworking and busy. Eddie would never have dared to disturb him, but Frayer had come to know Eddie by sight. One Sunday, Frayer came up to Eddie and asked his name. "You hang around here every Sunday," he said. "What do you want, anyway?"

"I want to help you build automobiles," Eddie told him. "Can I have a job?"

To Frayer, Eddie must have appeared a wiry, puny kid. Eddie was a lanky boy and had not yet acquired the husky build of his brother, Bill. Frayer shook his head and told Eddie he didn't have anything for him to do.

Despite the apparent rejection, Eddie was not going to let go of his desire so easily. Even if Frayer told him there was nothing to do, Eddie saw it differently. If nothing else, Frayer needed someone to clean up his messy and dirty shop. He confidently told Frayer that he had a job to do and would return the following morning.

Eddie showed up at the Frayer factory at seven the next morning. He didn't bother telling Evan's he had another job. Perhaps he was too focused on his new endeavor. Eddie found a broom and floor brush and went straight to work sweeping machines, benches, and floors. Mr. Frayer walked in at about 8:30 A.M. and saw the job Eddie had done. He looked around in approval and told Eddie that he'd got himself a job.

During his first few months at Frayer, Eddie not only cleaned but helped make carburetors, engine assemblies, and other parts of the automobiles. Every spare minute and break was devoted to his correspondence studies. His varying jobs provided hands-on experience for his lessons. Frayer took careful notice of Eddie's enthusiasm and ambition in his studies. One afternoon, he moved Eddie into the engineering department. This move opened up a new world to Eddie—the world of automobile design and creation. Eddie saw a one-dimensional object metamorphosize into metal reality.

Eddie also kept a tight eye on the racing cars developing at the Frayer factory. Mr. Frayer planned to race the three autos in the fall of 1906. The design of those cars was dedicated to speed and endurance. The racing cars consisted of little more than an engine, frame, and bucket seats. As the race drew closer, the workers began discussing past competitions and their winners.

As patriotic as Eddie was, it was common knowledge that the European cars often won the race. The European automotive industry was years ahead of the American industry in creating cars with sturdiness and speed. However, Frayer knew that if one of his cars placed, it meant more than victory. It meant business, and a lot of it.

The day Frayer and his engineers were scheduled to leave for New York City, Frayer told Eddie he wanted him to come along. Eddie ran home and then back, ready to go and filled with excitement. Seeing New York City for the first time would be thrilling in itself, but it was no comparison to attending his first automobile race.

In New York, Eddie's thrill grew to a full crescendo when Frayer asked him to ride with him in his car as his personal mechanic. Eddie would need to watch the oil gauge and gas gauge of the cars during the race. If either gauge showed a loss of pressure, Eddie would have to pump them back up. Eddie also needed to pay attention to the tires. If the tires started to

Eddie took part in his first car race in 1906 as Lee Frayer's mechanic. The race brought Eddie to New York for the first time, and marked the beginning of a long and successful racing career.

wear, Eddie would need to tell Frayer to stop and change them. When a tire wore down, the fabric underneath was a different color, so it would be easy for Eddie to see when they needed changing. The last thing Eddie had to do was to let Frayer know when someone wanted to pass him, since rearview mirrors had not yet been invented.

For several days before the race, Eddie and Frayer drove trial runs around the track. Frayer wanted to know what to watch for during the race and how his car handled around the turns. In the straightaways, Frayer opened up to speeds exceeding 70 miles per hour at times. The drivers of the other two cars practiced as well. After the practice runs, all three cars seemed to be working at top performance.

As the day of the race neared, Eddie was enthralled by the competitors. Other cars from the United States were entered in the race, as well as cars from Germany, France, England, and Italy. Some of the foreign cars included the French Panhard and Darracq, the German Mercedes, and the Italian Fiat. Only five entries per nation were allowed. On September 22, Frayer and his other two cars would compete in the elimination race. The top five U.S. cars would represent the United States in the Vanderbilt Cup Race.

Participating in the race with Frayer was an inspiration to Eddie. For more than four years he had been fatherless. Eddie respected Frayer, and the fact that Frayer took an intense interest in Eddie provided him with intense motivation to prove his ability and skill.

On the day of the elimination race, Frayer lined his car up with the others. The starter waved at each car, indicating it was their turn to pull onto the track. When Frayer's turn came, he let out the clutch and slammed the accelerator down. Eddie's eyes jumped from gas gauge to oil gauge. Everything looked in the green, and Eddie felt sure they would win the race. Frayer pushed the car as hard as he could. On one turn, however, he pushed a little too hard and a rear tire blew out. They quickly changed the tire and got back in the race.

After a short time back on the track, Eddie noticed the temperature gauge was reading in the red. He saw Frayer's eyes watching it as well. Eddie checked the oil pressure, but it seemed fine. The engine began making a faint knocking sound. As the car began losing power, there was nothing either of them could do to save it. The knocking grew louder. Finding it difficult to give up, Frayer continued to drive the track as long as he could. Other cars whizzed by them as Frayer finally pulled to the side and turned off the ignition. The two of them sat in silence at the side of the track for a long moment. Then Frayer sighed and simply said, "We're through."

Thus Eddie Rickenbacker's first race ended as quickly as it

had begun. But the event created an insatiable hunger in Eddie for racing. In the years to come, Eddie would get much more track time than he did as Lee Frayer's mechanic.

Even though Frayer's car was out of the race, one of the Frayer-Miller cars survived the elimination race and competed for the Vanderbilt Cup. In the seventh lap, however, the crankshaft broke. That was the end of the race for the Frayer-Miller Company, and it was the last race for Lee Frayer. About a year later, Frayer was offered a position as chief engineer of the Columbus Buggy Company. It was an offer that held too much promise to pass up.

When he told Eddie that he was leaving, he said, "I'd like to take you over there with me." Again, Eddie was presented with an opportunity that would keep him on the heels of a fast-changing industry. "We're going to build a brand-new automobile, and I'd like your help," Frayer said.

Eddie didn't have to think even for a minute. "I'll go with you, Mr. Frayer," he said.

The Racing
Years

A t age 17, Eddie was placed in charge of the experimental department at Columbus Buggy Company. This area of the company
supervised final testing of the high-wheeled motor buggy. Eddie
earned a salary of $20 a week, which was a great deal of money to him.

He spent countless hours testing the buggies, driving them
through the streets of Columbus and across the Ohio countryside.
He formed a relationship with those cars, and knew the ins and
outs of them. Much of his knowledge came to him the hard way.
For example, on one test run, while Eddie was cruising down a
steep hill, the brakes failed. Eddie saw that the road made a sharp
left curve at the bottom of the hill. His only option was to try to
make the turn. As carefully as he could and without panic, Eddie
tried to ease the speeding car around the turn, but the wheels did
not have enough play in them. The car flipped over, throwing
Eddie from the driver's seat. He hit the ground and the car flipped

over the top of him. Amazingly, Eddie stood up and walked away unharmed.

At times, Eddie would push a car to its breaking point. He would repeatedly take a buggy around a curve, each time increasing his speed. Eventually the increased speed would cause a wheel to snap off. Eddie thus learned not only the

Eddie toured the country in 1909, selling the new Firestone-Columbus. He proved to have an eye for more than just mechanics when he offered to drive presidential candidate William Jennings Bryan in Texas, earning valuable publicity for the FC.

maximum speed of performance for the buggies, but also how to repair the cars after they broke down.

He also learned that cars handle differently in varying types of weather. Eddie had begun traveling throughout the United States selling a new touring car called the Firestone-Columbus (FC). While the FC ran like a dream in Columbus, Ohio, it did not hold up so well in the intense heat of Dallas, Texas. Eddie discovered that by pouring cold water on the engine when it overheated, he could shrink the pistons a microscopic amount, making them functional even in hot weather.

While in Texas, Eddie saw an opportunity for Firestone-Columbus publicity. Presidential candidate William Jennings Bryan had stopped in Abilene, and Eddie offered to drive him while he was in town. Bryan accepted. As crowds gathered to see the candidate, they saw him riding in a brand new Firestone-Columbus. Eddie wrote to his mother in a letter dated December 1, 1909, "I personly [sic; all misspellings from original letter] drove William Jenings Brian the famous presidential candidate and champien of the little man to his lecture and the parade in his honor with thousands waching. My picture was on the front page of the Abilene Bee, and maybe all over Texas."

Eddie's fix-anything reputation landed him numerous traveling ventures for his company. In each instance, Eddie found a way to keep the cars running and make sales. Within two years, Eddie was promoted to a branch manager, pulling down a monthly salary of $150. But this wasn't enough to keep Eddie satisfied. In 1910, dirt-track racing was becoming increasingly popular throughout the Midwest. Eddie's attention was naturally drawn to this daring new sport, and he quickly found a way to work his overwhelming excitement for the sport into his current employment: What better way to draw the public's attention to the Firestone-Columbus than to race one of the company's cars in local dirt-track races? Eddie convinced Frayer to let him drive a new model in an upcoming race. The model was a small sports car powered by a four-cylinder high-speed engine, the first of its kind to be built in America. Eddie spent his nights stripping one of the cars down, reinforcing the frame, and getting it suited up for a 25-mile event in Red Oak, Iowa.

Eddie remembered how Frayer had memorized the track for the Vanderbilt Cup Race, and he followed that example. He tested his car against the curves and felt confident by the time race day came around.

Eddie jumped to an early lead. Lap after lap, he continued to pile into the curves without letting up on his speed. With all that continual pressure on the wheels, something was bound to give. Sure enough, going into one of the curves, a wheel gave way. The car plowed through the fence before rolling several times, throwing Eddie clear. Only a little dazed from the tumble, Eddie stood up and proceeded to check on the damage to his car. He wanted to see what repairs needed to be made before the next race. Eddie Rickenbacker would not be easily deterred.

The Fastest Competitor in the Grandstand

Eddie raced in Omaha, Nebraska, during Aksarben (Nebraska spelled backward) Week. Two days of the festival were devoted to auto racing, a feature event. Eddie entered every event possible, which amounted to ten races of varying lengths in those two short days. On the first day, Eddie took first place in all five events he entered. On day two, Eddie won the first four races. At the request of two competitors, Eddie agreed to pull out of the fifth race: The drivers for the Chalmers dealer and the Cadillac dealer had private bets going, but neither of them could collect if Eddie kept winning. The two bettors gave Eddie the first-place money. Eddie later recalled, "[It was] the only time I ever won sitting in the grandstand." Eddie collected $1,500 in those two days, $200 of which he paid to his mechanic.

During the summer of 1910, Eddie raced all over Nebraska and Iowa, winning more races than he lost. His champion car company benefited from Eddie's hobby as well. Before one Iowa race, a prospective buyer was having some difficulty making up his mind whether or not to purchase a Firestone-Columbus from Eddie. Eddie took first place in four out of five races driving the car on which the man was deciding. After the race, he told Eddie, "I want that car! When can you deliver it?"

Although Eddie was thrilled with racing, it sometimes involved considerable danger. Accidents were common on the crudely constructed tracks. Eddie was involved in several of them, but always escaped with only a few bruises and scrapes.

In 1911, Lee Frayer asked Eddie to enter a three-day race at the new Indianapolis Speedway, which had opened in 1909. Although the two knew that there was little hope of winning the fierce competition, Frayer still wanted to try, and he wanted Eddie as his relief driver. Eddie was excited to get the chance to compete against the big racing names of the day, including Wild Bob Burman, Spencer Wishart, Ralph De Palma, and Louis Chevrolet.

As the May 30 race date drew near, all the talk centered around one man, Ray Harroun. Harroun would be driving without a ride mechanic, using a new contraption he had designed: a rearview mirror. This was the world's first exposure to the device.

When the race began at ten in the morning, Frayer was at his car's wheel. Later, Eddie took over. While he was driving, the car in front of him, driven by Art Greiner, came to sudden halt. The jerk threw Greiner's mechanic from the car and to his death. This incident was the first time Eddie had ever seen a person die during a race. At the end of the 400-mile race, Harroun took first place; Eddie and Frayer took eleventh.

With the excitement of the big-time racing world hot in his blood, Eddie found it difficult to return to car sales and the dirt tracks of Nebraska. But he held out for another year. Frayer gave his Red Wing racing car to Eddie to use in the 1912 Indianapolis

Speedway race. Eddie did not place in the race, but it was after this event that he decided to leave his job with the Columbus Buggy Company. In Eddie's opinion, the company was not making an aggressive enough move into the automobile industry. As it turned out, Eddie's prediction was accurate. The company eventually went out of business.

Eddie knew he wanted to race, so he approached a company that was primed for innovation and growth. For a year or so, Eddie had been keeping a close eye on the Mason Automobile Company located in Des Moines, Iowa. The chief engineer of the company was Fred Duesenberg, a young man in his twenties. Eddie thought him brilliant, and that his automobiles reflected that genius.

On the day Eddie sent his resignation to the Columbus Buggy Company, he bought a one-way railroad ticket to Des Moines. He strolled into the Mason Company office and asked Duesenberg for a job. Duesenberg's racing cars still had a long way to go to completion, so he did not immediately need a driver. But Eddie's mechanical experience persuaded Duesenberg to hire him as a mechanic. So, Eddie left his $150-a-month sales position for a job that paid only $3 a day. But for Eddie, it was a leap into the world of automobile racing.

In 1913, Duesenberg's automobile company was teetering on the edge of business failure. Poor but determined, Duesenberg put together a racing team for the Sioux City race in Iowa, placing Eddie at the lead. The team worked day and night preparing the cars. Eddie was a hard-driving captain, but he quickly won the respect and adoration of the other members. In one race, the rubber tore loose from Eddie's rear tire. With each revolution, the rubber lashed at Eddie's arm. The riding mechanic put his arm out in back of Eddie's, taking the blow instead and leaving Eddie free to drive.

Before the Sioux City race, Eddie gathered up enough money to take a trip home to visit his mother. He went into great detail explaining to her Duesenberg's challenges for the

Eddie quit his job with the Columbus Buggy Company and signed on as a mechanic with the Mason Company, a move that gave him the opportunity to race. Races were often dangerous, and racers were challenged by the new technology of their vehicles as well as flying debris on the track.

upcoming race. In response, Elizabeth pulled out a book of Swiss folklore and began searching for a cure to her son's racing problems. In it she found a recipe for success: She told Eddie to tie a bat's heart to his middle finger with a piece of red silk thread. As silly as it sounded, Eddie was willing to try anything. After all, they had tried everything else.

Back in Sioux City, at a local farm, Eddie offered a silver dollar to the first child who brought him a live bat. The night before the race, one of the boys complied. The following morning, Eddie performed the surgery and tightly tied the bat's heart to his finger. Eddie later wrote, "I was invincible. Let the race begin!"

The Sioux City race was a major event, covered heavily by the press. The track was what Eddie referred to as "gumbo." The cars would tear up chunks of dried dirt, so hard they hit like rocks. The press joked "that anyone who survived the race would win it."

Eddie started the race strongly. He pushed his way to the front of the pack, and with five laps to go, he held a slight lead. As he guided the car around a curve, Eddie noticed the oil pressure was low. He nudged his riding mechanic, Eddie O'Donnell, with his elbow and pointed at the oil pressure. When he hit the next straightaway, the pressure had dropped even lower. Eddie wondered why O'Donnell wasn't pumping the oil.

Eddie glanced over his shoulder and felt his heart skip a beat. O'Donnell was slumped over with a bruise darkening his forehead. A "gumbo" rock must have hit him, knocking him out cold. The race was now up to Eddie alone to finish.

While holding tight to the steering wheel with one hand, Eddie reached back and gave the oil handle a few pumps. He kept his eye on the fast-approaching finish line. Against the odds, Eddie made it, winning by a slim forty seconds. Another member of the team came in third, bringing their prize money to a whopping $12,500. To everyone's relief, O'Donnell regained consciousness in the pit. Eddie wasn't sure whether to attribute the victory to the great Duesenberg engine or to the bat's heart still tied around his finger. Either way, the end result remained the same; the team was rich. In celebration, Eddie treated the team to a fine dinner and a night's stay in Sioux City's grandest hotel.

Eddie stayed with the Duesenberg team for two years, after which he decided it was time to go solo. After two unsuccessful independent races, Eddie unloaded his car to another driver. He then joined a three-man team, racing with two well-known drivers of the time—Barney Oldfield and Bill Carlson. The team drove for Maxwell Automobile Company. Eddie's job was to start off the race strong and aggressive in an attempt to wear out the competitors. After Eddie gained a commanding lead, the other two drivers would finish the race. This team union was the height of Eddie's golden racing years.

One of Eddie's most exciting races took place in Providence, Rhode Island. The event consisted of 100 laps around a one-mile asphalt track. Eddie did much preparation for the race, and while running practice laps, he discovered that heavier tires could last out the race. Most race-car drivers used small tires because a car could reach higher speeds with them, but Eddie found he could hold a steady speed of 80 miles per hour with the heavy tires.

On the day of the race, Eddie drove his warm-up laps using the small tires. Just before the race began, Eddie and his crew changed the tires to the heavier ones. Once again, Eddie raced against Wild Bob Burman. His tire choice paid off. The race came down to a back and forth battle between Burman and Eddie. The two drivers were nose to nose when Burman's tires wore out, and he had to make a pit stop. When Burman pulled out on the track again, he pushed his car to the limit, passing Eddie. But Eddie maintained his 80-mile-per-hour speed. Before long, Burman's second set of tires began to give, and he did not dare to take the curves too fast. Eddie passed him in the 98th lap and collected $10,000 in first-place prize money.

Eddie's name soon became front-page news. Sportswriters dubbed him with many nicknames, including the "Speedy Swiss," the "Baron," and the "Dutch Demon." At times, reporters invented stories and details about Eddie's life, including one article that claimed Eddie was a German baron. He learned to shrug them off.

Racing taught Eddie many valuable life lessons. Particularly, he learned the value of sportsmanship. He later wrote, "I figured that I could not win them all, so I might as well accept with good grace those that I lost." Eddie also became grateful for his safety through many close calls. One night, he had a dream that he was in a crash from which there was no escape. He awoke just moments before his demise and came to the realization that he was a very fortunate man.

Though he was a very religious man, Eddie was not necessarily so in the public eye. Many racing fans would have been surprised to know that he bent down on his knees each night to pray. But he continued to do so, and more. He decided to show the Lord his appreciation for keeping him in good health by exercising. For fifteen minutes each morning, Eddie performed a series of exercises to keep his body flexible.

During his racing years, Eddie gave himself a middle name. He wanted to add a little more color to his name, and what better way to do it than with a middle initial. He wrote his signature over and over, testing it with different initials. He finally decided on Edward V. Rickenbacker. To Eddie, this name was most pleasing to the eye. Of course, he then had to choose a name to accompany the letter. He chose Vernon.

Eddie's racing career took a turn in 1916. Maxwell decided to get out of the racing arena, which meant that Eddie was out of a job. Although he had saved some money, he didn't have enough to operate a racing team alone. So he put together a team with the "Four Horsemen" who had created the Indianapolis Speedway. The four men also formed the Prest-O-Life Company. Eddie ran this team as smoothly as he ran his cars; he compiled a rulebook and practiced pit drills with his team.

His efficient pit helped him take first place in a race in Tacoma, Washington. He beat Ralph De Palma by thirty seconds. Eddie wrote, "If my crew had taken as long in the pit as [De Palma's] did, he would have won that $10,000."

Eddie continued to live "life on the edge" during his racing. He endured many crashes, flips, bumps, and bang-ups. His daredevil approach to the racetrack won some big races for his team. In one, Eddie saw Carl Limberg and his mechanic thrown to their deaths in an accident. In his position right behind Limberg, Eddie saw the whole thing, but the drivers behind Eddie did not. By the time the trail of cars reached the accident site a second time, orange flames were blazing around the car. A billowing cloud of black smoke covered the track. Race officials waved at the drivers to proceed with caution at their own risk. Most slowed down to a crawl to avoid becoming a part of the accident themselves. But because Eddie had seen the accident, he knew the exact location of the demolished car. He pushed his accelerator down and sped through the dense smoke. His position at the time of the accident helped to earn him $25,000 in first-place prize money.

Eddie's most exciting race at the Indianapolis Speedway took place on Labor Day, 1916. The person Eddie wanted to beat was Johnny Aitken, who was driving the same car Eddie gave up early in his solo career. In the first part of the race, Eddie and Aitken held to each other like glue. Aitken then had to make a pit stop, which gave Eddie a half-mile lead. Both cars were running hard when a spoke on Eddie's right wheel popped. Before long, others were popping as well. Eddie knew the tire wouldn't last, and his pit crew had the same fear as they waved Eddie to stop. The officials too tried to wave Eddie down. Even Aitken tried to stop Eddie by pointing at the tire. But Eddie was determined to finish that race. Eddie later recalled that he felt no fear at the time.

He was on the last stretch when the tire blew. The car began to spin wildly. When it stopped, it was pointing toward the finish line. Eddie kept driving on the brake drums. As he crossed the finish line, the crowd was standing and cheering. Eddie looked back to see Aitken guiding his wounded car over the line. He had beat Aitken.

The official told Eddie, "That was the most spectacular show I have ever seen on this course."

Eddie replied, "I hope you never see one like it again."

In November 1916, Eddie was driving near Riverside, California, when he noticed an airplane parked in a field. Eddie pulled over to get a closer look. An early student of the Wright Brothers walked up to Eddie and introduced himself as Glenn Martin. Martin told Eddie that he owned the plane. As the two men peered into the two-seated plane, Martin asked Eddie if

Glenn Martin, seen here in a plane he designed and built around 1911, gave Eddie his first taste of flying. Eddie was thrilled by the 30-minute flight, which he found even more exciting than car racing.

he'd like to take a ride. Without a moment's hesitation, Eddie climbed into the rear seat of the plane.

Once in the air, Eddie was surprised he did not get dizzy. They stayed in the air for about thirty minutes. Just staying up in the air was a terrific feat in the early days of airplane travel, so Martin did not take Eddie through any fancy maneuvers. Eddie was fascinated by the trip, which provided an even greater rush than race-car driving.

On another occasion, Eddie was driving through the country-side when he saw a single-seater military plane in the middle of a cow pasture. The pilot was standing outside the plane, poking around in the engine. Eddie pulled over to see if he needed any help. The pilot was Major T. F. Dodd of the Army Air Service.

Knowing a thing or two about engines, Eddie offered to listen to the engine. He identified the problem as the ignition system and quickly fixed it. The major thanked Eddie and was on his way. Eddie later recalled, "I did not know how valuable that chance meeting with Major Dodd was going to prove before too long."

During the winter of 1916–1917, Eddie accepted an offer to race in Europe. Englishman Louis Coatalen of Sunbeam Motor Works wanted Eddie to help him prepare his cars. Coatalen made Eddie a fair offer for his work, and the trip would be all expenses paid. Eddie agreed to go abroad with his racing career.

When he sailed to England, World War I was underway in Europe. Although the United States had not yet entered the war, Eddie was well informed and knew about the events taking place overseas. He traveled on a small ship named the *St. Louis*. When he arrived in Liverpool, Eddie was pulled aside and questioned by British agents.

Apparently, these British agents had read the article that had said Eddie was a German baron. Thus he was suspected of being a German spy. Eddie calmly answered their questions and expressed his loyalty to the Allied cause, but it wasn't enough to convince the agents. After Eddie was searched, the agents then informed him that he could not enter England. He would have to stay on the ship until it returned to the United States. And he would not be allowed to contact Louis Coatalen.

After several long, stuffy days, the ship's captain agreed that Eddie could go ashore for Christmas Eve. Of course, he could not go unaccompanied; two British agents walked everywhere with him, flanking either side. The three men took separate rooms at the Adelphia Hotel in Liverpool. Eddie's room was in the middle, and no sooner would Eddie open his door than the other two would exit theirs.

Eddie ate a lonely dinner in his room but refused to spend his night of semifreedom cooped up. He strolled down the street from the hotel with his trusty companions following behind. The streets were lit only by a dim blue light on each corner. At the end of one block, Eddie turned down a side street and began running. He wasn't quite sure why he did this, except that it was his impulse at the moment. He ducked into an alley and watched the two agents pound past.

Eddie yelled to them, "Hey, here I am." He later commented, "It was a wonder they did not shoot me."

By the time the agents returned, Eddie had worked himself up to a rolling laughter. The agents lightened their moods and began laughing as well. Eddie then offered to buy them a beer at a nearby tavern. The agents agreed, and the three men enjoyed an evening of stories and laughs.

After Christmas Eve, Eddie had pretty much convinced the agents that he was not a spy. On Christmas Day, Eddie got to make his call to Coatalen and was soon free to meet him. Once again, Eddie put in long hours and hard work for Sunbeam. His hotel room overlooked the Thames River, and Eddie excitedly watched military training planes fly over the river. He decided then that if ever he was to serve his country, it would be in aviation.

On February 3, 1917, the United States broke off its European relations and all Americans traveling abroad had five days to leave. That announcement ended Eddie's work with the Sunbeam racing team. He met his old friends, the British agents, at the *St. Louis*, and was on his way home.

To the Skies

Back in the United States, Eddie turned his efforts to supporting United States involvement in the Allied cause. He began touring the country, giving speeches, and pushing for public support. As a former race-car driver, he drew quite a crowd and considerable press. His slogan was "The Three M's—Men, Money, Munitions." He spoke in New York, Columbus, Detroit, Chicago, and Los Angeles.

As Eddie continued to make his speeches, he also made plans to become one of the "Men" in his three M's. In particular, Eddie was eager to join the flying squadron. And if the squadron did not work out, Eddie was certain he would somehow find a way to become a military aviator and have an opportunity to serve his country. Unfortunately, the military felt it was a poor idea to commission ex-race-car drivers as military pilots. In addition, military officials were looking for men under 25, with a college education. Although three strikes

To the Skies | 53

To the Skies | 53

usually meant you were out, 27-year-old Rickenbacker was not about to give up.

In the meantime, Eddie needed to find some work. During his traveling campaign for Allied support, Eddie had depleted much of his savings. He decided to prepare a car to race in the Memorial Day 500, which was to take place in Cincinnati, Ohio, in May 1917. One day, driver Jack LeCain and his daughter, Mary Alice, visited Eddie. Mary Alice presented Eddie with an identification card and a crucifix, secured in a leather folder.

"As long as you carry it with you, you won't be shot or

Eddie used his notoriety as a race-car driver to support the Allied effort, calling for "Men, Money, and Munitions." But Eddie was eager to take to the skies as a fighter pilot to defend the United States.

anything like that," Mary Alice explained. Eddie smiled and thanked the girl. He carefully pushed the little folder in his upper left-hand coat pocket. When his jacket lay flat, the folder directly protected his heart. Eddie wrote, "Since then I have never, not one day in more than fifty years, gone out without making sure that her little talisman is in that pocket."

After practicing on the track one night in May, Eddie received a phone call in his hotel room. On the other end was an old friend, Major Burgess Lewis. He was phoning Eddie from New York and told him that the military was organizing a secret sailing to France. They needed staff drivers, and he wondered if Eddie would be interested in such a mission.

Eddie told Lewis that he'd like to think about it overnight and asked him to call back in the morning. All night, Eddie weighed the pros and cons of the offer. At this time, no troops had been sent to France, although the United States had officially entered the war on April 6. Eddie had believed it was possible to bypass the regulations that excluded him from the military in the United States if he could get overseas, where the fighting was. He finally decided that if he didn't go on this mission, he may never have another chance to serve his country, especially taking into consideration that he had already been suspected as a German spy. The next morning, Eddie told Lewis he would join right after the race.

Lewis chuckled and told Eddie, "If you aren't in New York tomorrow morning, Eddie, there's no use of your coming at all." Eddie told Lewis that he'd be there.

By noon the next day, Eddie was a sergeant in the U.S. Army. He then sailed the following day with the American Expeditionary Force. Eddie's billet was in steerage, the filthiest part of the ship. Eddie slept in a hammock and the tables on which he ate crawled with bugs. Later in the day, Eddie learned that there were different classes of sergeants, and the higher the class, the better the billet.

It turns out that also sailing on the ship was aviation officer

Colonel T. F. Dodd, the man whose plane Eddie fixed. Eddie went straight to Colonel Dodd to discuss the matter of his accommodations. He told Dodd frankly that he would like a promotion. Colonel Dodd explained that promotions are awarded by meritorious service and asked Eddie how he planned to go about that.

"I don't know, Colonel," Eddie told him, "that's why I brought you along."

The Colonel burst into laughter and promoted Eddie to sergeant first class. Compared to steerage, Eddie's new second-class cabin provided heavenly accommodations. But he didn't forget his partners in steerage. With a little Rickenbacker charm, he convinced the cook to deliver a basket of food and fresh fruit daily to the men in steerage.

After their arrival in Liverpool, Eddie was on a mission with Colonel Dodd when the two came upon a stalled automobile. Like a true trained mechanic, Eddie immediately identified the problem and had the car running before long. The officer who drove the vehicle was thoroughly impressed with Eddie's expertise. This incident was Eddie's first encounter with William "Billy" Mitchell, America's famous air pioneer. After that day, Mitchell, who continued to be impressed with Eddie's fix-all talent, often requested Eddie for his driver.

One afternoon in Paris, Eddie saw James Miller, a New York banker and a friend of Eddie's who was also serving in the U.S. military. Miller told him that he was soon to be put in charge of the advanced flying school at Issoudun. Needing an engineer, he told Eddie he'd like him on board. Eddie explained to Jim that he would be glad to do his best, but it would probably be beneficial if the engineering officer of a flying school knew how to fly. Miller told Eddie he'd see what he could do.

Miller made a formal request for Eddie's services to Colonel Mitchell. Colonel Mitchell asked Eddie if he really wanted to fly. "Yes, sir," Eddie responded emphatically. "Anybody can drive this car. I'd appreciate the opportunity to learn to fly."

Mitchell found a way around the red tape for Eddie. The doctor who performed the physical turned out to be a racing enthusiast and miraculously made Eddie two years younger. He recorded Eddie's birthdate as October 8, 1892, making Eddie 25 years old; his true age would have disqualified him.

In Tours, France, Eddie learned how to fly. After two short flights with an instructor, it was time for Eddie to take to the air solo. He was scared to death. He also had some difficulty squeezing into a cockpit that was designed for a small-framed man and not the six-foot-two Rickenbacker.

A strong crosswind was blowing. At the beginning of the run, Eddie was tense, trying to gauge the right moment to lift the tail. Feeling the pressure from the crosswind, he pushed down on the left rudder. He overcompensated and the plane turned straight for the hangar. The instructors and other students who were out watching scattered in every direction. Eddie pushed down on the right rudder, and the tail swung around, missing the hangar by several feet. Once again, Eddie headed out to the grassy field, and this time he was going to get it right. Sure enough, as Eddie pulled back on the stick, the plane lifted into the air.

Eddie's flight training lasted a slim 17 days. After 25 hours of flying time, Eddie walked away a pilot and a first lieutenant in the Signal Corps. With his training complete, he reported at Issoudun as an engineering officer. Between jobs, Eddie would catch an occasional lecture and pick up any extra knowledge he could. He continued to take a small plane out for flight practice as well.

For some time, Eddie had overheard the instructors and student pilots talking about the tailspin. This maneuver was difficult, but it was a valuable stunt because it made the plane hard to hit in combat. In a tailspin, the pilot stalls the plane, then gives the rudder a hard kick. The nose drops, and the tail begins spinning around. The challenge was too much for Eddie to resist; he just had to learn how to do a tailspin.

At first, Eddie was extremely cautious. The move wasn't only difficult, it was frightening. He started with only a single revolution, but soon worked his way up to a beautiful, long tailspin that he could bring close to the ground. As he listened to the young pilots brag about the number of revolutions they could make, Eddie kept quiet. Instead, he decided to make his "tailspin debut" during a Sunday football game.

Eddie waited until the football game was in progress. He then flew high over the field, stalled the plane, and began a tailspin over the center of the field. As he neared the ground, players and spectators dashed for cover. Eddie pulled out of the spin just in time. The commander, Major Spaatz, grounded Eddie for a month over the incident. But, as Eddie recalled, "I sure broke up that ball game."

In January 1918, the first group of pilots who had finished training at Issoudun was ordered to the school of aerial gunnery at Cazeau in southern France. This school was the final step before going into combat. Eddie examined the list of names, but did not see his own. He questioned Major Spaatz, who told Eddie that he was too important at the school.

Eddie was not about to take no for an answer. Combat was why he had sailed to Europe, and in combat was where he was determined to be. To prove to Major Spaatz that the school would run just fine without him, he went to the school surgeon with a cold and asked to be hospitalized for two weeks. After the two weeks, Eddie went to see Major Spaatz again. Without speaking a word, Major Spaatz handed Eddie orders to report to Cazeau. Eddie thanked the major but asked why the change of heart.

"I'm on to your little game, Rickenbacker," Major Spaatz told him. "But if your heart's set on going to Cazeau, you're no damn good to me around here." He wished Eddie the best of luck.

At Cazeau, Eddie learned how to handle gunnery. He mastered his shot with a 30-caliber rifle and a machine gun. Finally, his training completed, he was officially a combat pilot with the skill to fly and to shoot. After a 10-day leave in Paris, Eddie was dispatched to the 94th Aero Pursuit Squadron in March 1918. This unit was the first American squadron to go into action on the western front.

Eddie's squadron was assigned to the aerodrome near Villeneuve, about 15 miles from the front lines. He was both honored and impressed to be in the presence of Major Raoul Lufbery, the American "Ace of Aces." Lufbery had shot down 17 enemy aircraft and was considered the greatest pilot.

The 94th was somewhat disappointed to find that their planes were Nieuports, French castoffs, and even more disturbing, they were not equipped with guns. While waiting for the guns to arrive, Eddie mustered up the courage to approach Major Lufbery. Aside from the honor Eddie felt just being in the major's company, he wanted an opportunity to learn from him. The major sensed Eddie's eagerness to learn and obliged him. The two airmen discussed every maneuver the Nieuports could make and every type of attack Eddie could encounter. Lufbery talked about a corkscrew maneuver he used when flying near enemy lines. When flying in a corkscrew motion, turning side to side, the pilot could see the skies in all directions and make mental notes of what he saw.

On March 6, Lufbery announced that he would lead a flight of three unarmed planes on a patrol over German lines. Out of the twenty pilots in the squadron, only two would be chosen. The silence that followed his announcement must have seemed like an eternity to those twenty young men. Lufbery's eyes met Eddie's. "Rick," he said casually, "you and Campbell be ready to leave at 8:15."

Before the team left, Eddie was reminded to be on the look-out for "Archie." In World War I, Archie was the name given to

Eddie joined the 94th Aero Pursuit Squadron after his training and was assigned to the aerodome near Villeneuve, just a short distance from the front line. He is seen here in a Nieuport plane, shortly after joining the squad.

antiaircraft fire. Because the group would be venturing over the German lines, it was altogether possible that they could be shot at by Germans on the ground.

In the air, Eddie tried to follow Lufbery's corkscrew path, but found it more difficult to perform than he had thought. And what was more, the side to side motion was making him airsick. Eddie tried to ignore the turning in his stomach, but a few moments later he broke into a cold sweat and felt the nausea welling up inside. Suddenly, there was a flash of light, and the plane shook violently. It was Archie. Eddie looked behind the plane and saw billows of black smoke dotting his trail. He was being shot at.

After the immediate moment of terror, Eddie realized that neither he nor his plane had suffered any damage. And in all the sudden excitement, his airsickness had left him. Eddie also learned a little something about himself: He had been shot at and did not panic. He had passed a personal test of fear and remained a true and dependable combat man.

Back on the ground, Eddie told his flying buddies about his experience. When they asked if he saw any enemy planes, Eddie responded that they had the sky to themselves. Of course, he told them all about Archie, but that his plane did not have a scratch to show for it.

Listening to Eddie's description of the flight, Major Lufbery asked him if he was certain there were no other planes in the sky. Eddie confirmed his initial report of "not a one." Shaking his head, Lufbery told Eddie that a formation of five Spads crossed beneath them before they passed the German lines. About fifteen minutes later, they passed another five Spads. And four German Albatroses were straight ahead of them when they turned to come back. "You must learn to look around," he told Eddie.

Lufbery paused and grinned at Eddie. He then walked over to Eddie's plane. Reaching out to the tail, he poked his finger through a bullet hole. He also pointed out a spot where shrapnel had penetrated both wings, just a foot away from the cockpit. It was a humbling moment for Eddie, but also a lesson in awareness for an amateur pilot.

The Nieuport 28 Fighter Plane

During World War I, Eddie flew a Nieuport 28 fighter plane. This aircraft was the first fighter plane flown in combat by pilots of the American Expeditionary Forces. At the time, the Nieuport was considered obsolete, inferior to the Nieuport 17 "Superbébé," but American pilots obtained more victories with the aircraft than they did losses. The Nieuport 28 was more maneuverable than some of the heavier fighter planes, such as the SPAD XIII, but it was more fragile, and in a dive would shed fabric from the upper wing.

Eddie continued tutoring sessions with Lufbery. He practiced the corkscrew move over and over, until he finally could perform it without getting sick. All the while, members of the 94th complained about the amount of time it was taking for them to get their guns. Eddie later wrote, "We were actually luckier than we realized. We were accumulating experience that would enable us to save our own skins and to shoot down our foes."

When the German spring offensive of 1918 began, the 94th moved to a safer location at Épiez, France. There, the squadron received their equipment, guns, ammunition, instruments, and flying clothing. Shortly after they received their supplies, they moved up to Toul, only 18 miles from the lines. Now that they were armed, Eddie thought for sure they would be the first American squadron to go into combat against the enemy. In honor of this event, the squadron created a special insignia. All of the pilots contributed their suggestions. The flight surgeon, Lieutenant Walters, reminded the men of the "old American custom of throwing a hat into a ring as an invitation to battle." Consequently, the Hat-in-the-Ring was born, becoming one of the world's most famous military insignias.

On the morning of April 14, 1918, Eddie took off with two other military aviators for a patrol of the lines near Toul with the Hat-in-the-Ring insignia emblazoned on his Nieuport plane. According to Eddie, this patrol was the first mission ever ordered by an American commander of an American squadron of American pilots. During Eddie's first few flights he learned numerous lessons about combat flight. On one flight, Eddie sighted an enemy plane over Saint-Mihiel. Eddie came on the enemy plane apparently unnoticed, despite the shell bursts that followed his path across the sky, courtesy of Archie. Several moments before he attacked, Eddie remembered the words of Major Lufbery—look out for a trap. Sure enough, coming in on top of him was a German Albatros. Eddie knew his little Nieuport could outclimb the heavy

Before becoming a flying ace, Eddie had a lot to learn about the hidden dangers of aerial combat. These two U.S. Air Force planes collide in midair during a battle, after the first plane was shot down and fell into the second plane. One of the pilots was able to parachute to safety (above right).

German fighter, and he managed to get away. He came back down on the enemy's tail when he remembered Lufbery's advice again. This time, Eddie saw two more planes coming at him. Eddie tried every maneuver he knew, but the planes stuck with him. Then, just ahead of him, Eddie saw a beautiful cloud. He flew directly into it, hiding himself. When he poked his nose out the other side, there was no sign of the planes. He returned to the field.

After he landed, Doug Campbell and Charley Chapman, two of Eddie's flying buddies, wondered why he was trying to run away from them. It turns out the pursuing "enemy" was actually Eddie's teammates. Eddie was disappointed by his inability to identify them in the air. It cost him his first air victory.

One day, Eddie and Captain Jimmy Hall lifted off in search of an enemy two-seater plane that had been reported flying south of the lines. They located the plane and got into position. Eddie prepared himself for his first combat experience. He felt his heard pounding in his chest and an image of a Liberty Bond poster popped into his head. The poster was of a beautiful girl with outstretched arms. Printed on the poster were the words, "Fight or Buy Bonds." Eddie decided he did not have much of a choice.

Eddie and Hall dived in on the Pfalz plane. Eddie pulled his triggers and hit the tail. He watched two streaks of fire move from the fuselage into the pilot's seat. Shortly after, the plane swerved, curved down, and crashed. Eddie earned his first victory and celebrated with his squadron back on the ground.

It was during this time that Eddie officially changed the spelling of his name to Rickenbacker, exchanging the German "h" for an all-American "k." Papers all over the United States reported that "Eddie Rickenbacker has taken the Hun out of his name." (Hun was a disparaging name for a German soldier.)

On one mission, south of Metz on the Moselle, Eddie spotted four Fokker D-7s. He climbed into the sunlight above the planes and let them pass beneath him. He then dived at them. At 50 yards, Eddie fired on the last plane and downed it. He later recalled, "The pilot never knew what hit him."

The other three planes turned to the right. As Eddie watched the sunlight bounce off their red noses, a chill slowly climbed up his spine. Those blood-red noses meant Eddie was up against the dreaded "Flying Circus" of Manfred von Richthofen, the Red Baron. Although the Red Baron himself was no longer alive, this famous squadron remained the epitome of flying excellence.

Manfred von Richthofen— The Red Baron and the Flying Circus

Manfred von Richthofen was born on May 2, 1892, in Schweidnitz. At age 11, Manfred attended the Wahlstatt Cadet School in Berlin, eager to be in the German military. As it turned out, Manfred disliked the rigid schedule, and he received poor grades. But he graduated into the Senior Cadet Academy, which he liked better. He went on to join the cavalry.

When World War I began in 1914, Manfred was 22 years old. At the beginning of the war, Manfred fought in the trenches. He would look up at the sky and admire the planes. What he really wanted was to fly. In 1915, Manfred began flying fighter planes for the German army. He quickly increased his abilities and skills and was on his way to becoming a flying ace.

In April 1917, "Bloody April," Manfred shot down 21 enemy aircraft. These victories brought his total to 52, breaking the German record of 40 victories. Manfred was the new ace of aces. He immediately became a hero. Postcards were printed with his image, and people all over the world told stories about his victories.

On June 24, 1917, Manfred became the commander of an elite flying squadron that became known as the Flying Circus. Flying Circus pilots flew red-painted Fokker planes (the Red Baron's plane was a Fokker Dr.I triplane), and any American fighter who came upon this unit knew that they were up against the best of the best. As commander of the Flying Circus, he became known as the Red Baron.

Flying in the Circus was not an easy task. Manfred faced many skilled Allied pilots. In early July, he experienced a narrow escape from a fight. He was attacking several pusher planes when he was shot. Manfred remembered, "Suddenly there was a blow to my head! I was hit! For a moment I was completely paralyzed. . . . My hands dropped to the side, my legs dangled in the fuselage. The worst part was that the blow on the head had affected my optic nerve and I was completely blind. The machine dived down." At about 2,600 feet, Manfred partially regained his sight. He was able to land the plane successfully, but suffered a bullet wound to the head. The injury put him out of the sky until mid-August.

As the war progressed, Manfred could sense that Germany's fate was grim. An energetic fighter at the start of the war, he became increasingly depressed and experienced some anxiety about death and battle. On April 20, Manfred shot down his 80th enemy aircraft, bringing his victories to an outstanding high. The following day, Manfred was shot down during a fight. A single bullet had entered through the right side of his back and exited two inches higher from his left chest. At age 25, Manfred was dead. No one knows for certain who fired the deadly bullet. At the time the plane went down, Manfred was being shot at by both ground fire and a British fighter.

The Flying Circus outnumbered Eddie three to one. Their fine flying pushed him to perform his maneuvers to perfection. There was no room for error. Eddie later wrote that he performed many of his fancy moves out of sheer fright. Suddenly the sky opened up beneath him, delivering an opportunity. Eddie turned his nose down and corkscrewed out of danger. Back on the ground, he proudly announced his first victory over the elite Flying Circus.

The next day, Eddie shot down another Fokker in the same area. This was his seventh victory, earning him the most envied war title—American Aces of Aces. Eddie had risked his life many times to achieve this honor. However, since the four other pilots who held that title were now dead, Eddie worried that the honor carried with it the curse of death.

During 1918, Eddie led numerous daring and successful missions, including another victory against the scarlet-nosed Flying Circus. On October 30, Eddie gained his 25th and 26th victories. On November 10, he led his squadron to what would be their last victory. Later that evening, Eddie sat with a group of pilots, planning out the next day's mission. The phone rang, and a nearly hysterical voice on the other end told Eddie that the following morning at 11:00, the war would be over. Eddie dropped the phone and turned to his pilots. "The war is over!" he shouted.

The men celebrated through the night, blasting firearms into the sky—star shells, rockets, parachute flares, and streams of lights. "What a night!" Eddie remembered.

Buying
an Airline

After the war, Eddie worked to readjust his life to serving mankind in peace, rather than through the destructiveness of war. During the previous several years, Eddie had been under a lot of pressure. He had endured 134 aerial encounters in which other human beings tried to shoot him out of the sky. Through Eddie's battles with the Grim Reaper, he recognized the Power which had brought him safely back home. Eddie wanted to take some time to reflect on his experiences and develop a plan for his future.

In late summer 1919, Eddie took a trip across the desert. He wandered aimless across the southwestern United States, without care or rush. At night, he slept out under the open sky, looking up into the dazzling expanse, dispensing of pressures and stabilizing his nerves. He understood that his life was changed forever. He held the title "American Ace of Aces," and with that title came responsibility. To many, Eddie Rickenbacker was a national hero. Whatever publicity would come from Eddie's service to his country, he vowed never to let his image be cheapened.

Before long, Eddie was approached by publishers, directors, and numerous promoters who wanted to use his image to sell their products. Eddie received offers from cigarette companies, clothing companies, and even a chewing gum company. Carl Laemmle, from Universal Studios, presented Eddie with a check for $100,000, hoping he would star in a movie.

Eddie was aware of his potential to influence America's youth. He wanted to set an example that would inspire the young, and he felt a motion picture was not the proper tool for inspiration.

On February 3, 1919, Eddie realized exactly how much his performance during World War I meant to his countrymen. In a speech, Secretary of War Newton D. Baker said these words: "[Eddie's] life will always be gladdened as he looks about him

Eddie, seen here with other members of the 94th Aero Squadron, stands proudly next to his Nieuport bearing the Hat-in-the-Ring insignia. Eddie's heroics were legendary, and he was approached by many after the war who wanted to use his image to sell their products.

and sees men and women and children walking about free and unafraid and when he thinks that he has given his best and ventured his own life to bring this about."

Eddie was then presented with a pair of jeweled wings in honor of his military service. Asked to respond, he simply held out his wings in his mother's direction and said, "For you, Mother." After he sat down, everyone attending the ceremony stood, some on their chairs and tables, and applauded. Eddie saw tears running down the cheeks of men and women alike. He felt the power of emotion alive in the room and accepted it as one of his greatest moments.

Later in the evening, Eddie spoke to Secretary Baker about a project to prove the feasibility of air transportation to the American public. He suggested organizing a transatlantic flight, but stressed that it could only be achieved through government resources. Baker politely told Eddie that the government did not care to fund such a project. The truth was that lack of foresight and mismanagement had placed a black mark on the overall American aviation effort during the war. America was far behind Germany, France, and Italy in aircraft technology. But despite these facts, Eddie was unable to spark Baker's interest.

He continued to push his dream for air travel through his touring speeches. At one talk in Seattle in August 1919, Eddie said, "I feel that I am living in a new era ten years hence, and that the North Star is actually the shining headlight of a large passenger plane just arriving from Alaska. . . . carrying an average of from two to three hundred passengers." The public did not foresee the same future for America, and most perceived his visions as crazy aspirations. A critic suggested that perhaps Eddie's ideas could be attributed to breathing all the thin air up in his plane. But Eddie continued to confidently speak about air travel. In 1920, Eddie took part in a cross-country tour to promote air travel.

Meanwhile, Eddie also turned his attention to the world of

Eddie is seen here with distributor George Morse outside a Rickenbacker Motor Company showroom in Minneapolis. Unfortunately, the company was short-lived and went out of business in 1927.

automobiles. From 1920 to 1927, he served as vice president of the Rickenbacker Motor Company. He directed sales for the company, which started out as a success, peaking at 1,200 distributors in 1922. However, the company soon began a decline and ended in bankruptcy in 1927.

The Rickenbacker Automobile

After the war, Eddie decided to build his own automobile, a dream he had turned over in his mind many times during his racing years. Eddie wanted to produce a car with a four-wheel brake system. From his years in racing, he knew how much better a car with this feature would handle. The car would be the first of its kind, which made other big companies nervous. Rickenbacker automobiles received a great deal of negative press prior to release. Competitors argued that the four-wheel brakes would be unsafe, causing the car to flip around turns.

Eddie designed and produced several models, and stamped them with a dependable name, Rickenbacker. He produced the "Super-sport" coupe, the "Vertical-8 Superfine" coupe-roadster, Brougham, Phaeton, and the six-cylinder sport Phaeton. At first Eddie's sales did well, but upon release of the four-wheel brake system, Eddie's dealers did a poor job in pushing the cars, and the sales rapidly declined. Rickenbacker Motors eventually went bankrupt.

Shortly after the war, Eddie attended a party in New York. There, he met Adelaide Frost Durant, a woman he had actually met in California before the war. At the party, Eddie asked her to dinner, and later, he took her to a New Year's Eve party. As Eddie described it, "Dan Cupid shot him down in flames." They were married on September 16, 1922, after which they honeymooned in Europe for six weeks.

Eddie and Adelaide had two sons: David Edward was born on January 4, 1925, and William Frost followed on March 16, 1928. Eddie did not want to name either one of his sons Edward, Jr. He never liked being called "Eddie" himself. To him, the name brought to mind a little fellow, and he saw to it that neither one of his sons would so named.

Just as Eddie predicted, the airline industry finally began to show potential. By 1928, routes totaling 35,000 miles were flown every day by airmail, transport, and passenger planes. On November 22, 1928, Eddie spoke before the Washington Board of

Trade on behalf of constructing a national airport in Washington, D.C. Speaking of air travel, Eddie said, "We are on the threshold of a new era. . . . See it, recognize it and grasp the opportunity it offers." Shortly after that speech, 450 acres of land was prepared for the site of Washington's National Airport.

In June 1929, Eddie accepted a position as vice president in charge of sales for Fokker Aircraft Company, which had recently been taken over by General Motors. His family immediately moved to New York, and he began work on July 1. Within his first several months at Fokker, Eddie helped negotiate the purchase of Pioneer Instrument Company, which made precision instruments for aircraft. This company later became known as the Bendix Aviation Company.

When the stock market crashed in 1929, the budding aviation industry took a heavy blow. Due to the economy, General Motors decided to move Fokker to Baltimore, renaming the company General Aviation, Inc. However, even though Eddie was thrilled to be a part of aviation growth, he did not want to move his family to Baltimore. He resigned in March 1932.

On April 29, 1932, Eddie joined Aviation Corporation. Aviation Corporation, or AVCO, was established in the late 1920s, when the exciting opportunity that aviation held became more apparent to the financial world. Brokers W. Averell Harriman and Robert Lehman organized the large holding company and with it gained several small airlines that were scattered across the United States. AVCO combined the airlines into one company called American Airways. Eddie became its vice president.

At this time, two major airlines controlled commercial travel. American Airways held the east-west travel routes, and the north-south operation was held by Eastern Air Transport. Eddie saw a huge benefit in merging the two companies. American Airways did the majority of its business in the eight months of spring, summer, and fall. The winter months were the busiest for Eastern Air Transport. If the two companies could get together, they would share a year-round peak.

Eastern Air Transport was owned by Clement M. Keys, who had created the huge holding company of North American Aviation, Inc. The Depression years had worn Keys down, and in 1933, he declared bankruptcy. Eddie saw this event as an incredible opportunity to snatch up Eastern Air Transport and gain control of the north-south routes. He suggested to AVCO management that they purchase North American Aviation, Inc.

But differences of opinion had caused factions to grow among the business leaders of AVCO. The conflicts resulted in the company director firing Harriman and Lehman. Being allied with these two businessmen, Eddie informed the company director that he would be handing in his resignation. The director asked Eddie to stay on long enough to finish his current duties, to which Eddie agreed. When, in February 1933, the company director moved the home office of American Airways to Chicago, Eddie used this as his excuse to "resign." His boys were in school in the New York area, and Eddie did not want to uproot his family.

Still operating with the knowledge that North American Aviation, Inc., was unclaimed, Eddie went on a search for a buyer. North American Aviation's holdings included stock in Pan American, TWA, and Western Air Express airlines, as well as ownership of Eastern Air Transport Company and Sperry Gyroscope—an impressive list. Naturally, Eddie's first thought for a potential buyer was General Motors, and soon the company's board of directors approved a move to purchase 30 percent of North American Aviation. Eddie was once again appointed as vice president.

In 1934, airline pilots flew daily routes to deliver airmail. Even though the airline industry was still in its youth in the United States, it was still flying 200,000 miles in a 24-hour period. Strict regulations applied for becoming a pilot of a commercial airline. A pilot was required to have at least 4,000 hours of flying time, and copilots had to have a minimum of 1,000. Pilots were highly experienced and familiar with their routes. They knew every mountain, tree, and building along their path and could navigate the route in rain or shine, day or night.

But, on February 9, 1934, Postmaster General James Farley announced that all airmail contracts with commercial airlines would be canceled, effective February 19. President Franklin D. Roosevelt announced several days later that the Army Air Service would fly the mail in military planes. Eddie was shocked and furious. He had much respect for military aviators, but they did not seem the proper replacement for experienced pilots with specialized equipment.

Just as Eddie had feared, three army pilots died in two plane crashes while reporting to their assigned stations to begin flying mail on the 20th. Two of the young men hit a mountaintop in Utah during a snowstorm. The other crashed due to fog in Idaho. Eddie declared, "That's legalized murder!" In 1934, Eddie cancelled his commission as colonel in the Specialist Reserve in protest of the airmail situation.

The National Broadcasting Company asked Eddie to make a fifteen-minute, coast-to-coast statement on Roosevelt's new mail order. Eddie hired an editor from the *Los Angeles Times* and the *Examiner*, to help him write a fiery speech. Eddie also made plans to accompany a transcontinental flight right after his speech to prove the reliability of a new plane, the DC-2.

Just as Eddie was getting ready to go to the airport to make his speech, he learned that Washington had ordered NBC to cut Eddie off the air if anything he said was controversial. That voided Eddie's speech, and he opted for a milder rendition. But he still successfully managed to sneak in a few controversial remarks. Eddie then boarded the DC-2 and flew from Los Angeles to Newark, New Jersey, in thirteen hours and two minutes. This flight was the first transport to fly across the continent with only two stops.

More military men were killed flying mail during the following weeks. Finally, Postmaster General Farley agreed to reassign airmail delivery to the airlines, but with conditions and exclusions. Due to some of the fine print, several airlines changed their names slightly to avoid being blacklisted. For example, Eastern Air Transport became Eastern Air Lines and American Airways became American Airlines.

Eddie took over the Eastern Air Lines company, which was in rough shape and losing money. Eddie knew the situation looked bad, but he could see potential. He also saw it as his patriotic duty to contribute to the building of the aeronautic enterprise. In Eddie's opinion, aviation would enhance the economy and allow the United States to create a stable national defense. In addition, Eddie had a dream to lift Eastern Air Lines out of government subsidy into a flight of free enterprise and self-sufficiency.

In Eddie's first year with Eastern Air Lines, the company made $38,000. It was a minute amount, but Eddie had proved success was within reach. When employees saw Eddie's contributions and dedication, morale was boosted and everyone pitched in to help.

One day in January 1938, Eddie received a phone call from a local newspaper. The journalist asked Eddie to comment on the proposed sale of Eastern Air Lines to John Hertz. Silence separated the two men for a moment, and Eddie replied, "I can't tell you anything about it. This is the first I've heard of it."

After the news sank in, Eddie was hurt and angry. He had spent the previous three years building the company to a profitable level. The company would be sold from underneath him for $3 million, less than what Eddie thought it was worth. Now he felt as though his reward was to be kicked out of his position, not to mention the fact that Eddie had developed relationships with his employees, who were part of his direct concern.

Eddie decided he needed to find a way to put in a higher offer for Eastern Air Lines. He contacted a few old friends in banking and managed to come up with $3.5 million. The offer was

Eddie was considering the future of aviation when he took over Eastern Air Lines, and correctly predicted that air travel and shipping would be a boon to the nation's economy.

accepted and Eddie became the owner and president of an airline.

Eddie made many pioneering advances in the airline industry. He established a medical department and required all pilots to undergo medical examinations. He organized a meteorology department to monitor the weather conditions. He also took a vested interest in his employees. He often stressed that it was "our" airline and valued their suggestions and complaints. In addition, he checked up on them. Often, the employees were right, and Eddie took measures to correct any problems.

It had been many years since Eddie had had a brush with death. He experienced two more such encounters, however, both while flying in the new DC-2. Once, while returning from California, a loud noise pulled Eddie up out of his seat.

Judging by the sound, Eddie assessed that a piece of the propeller blade had broken off and hit the fuselage. The right engine began vibrating.

"Shut it off! Shut it off!" Eddie yelled to the pilot and copilot. But they didn't seem to hear him. The noise continued. Eddie hollered again and again, and after several seconds, the right engine was finally cut. They landed the plane in Columbus, and Eddie talked to the pilot. Apparently, the plane was on autopilot when the propeller broke. Upon landing, Eddie found out that the commotion in the engine broke several mounts, and the right engine was being held on by only one support. Because the pilot was not in control of the plane, he did not immediately realize what had happened. His delay could have cost the lives of everyone on board. Many years passed before Eastern Air Lines again used automatic pilots.

Eddie's second encounter with the Grim Reaper happened in the middle of winter. He was accompanying an inaugural flight for the opening of a Chicago–Miami route. The weather during the flight turned inclement—snow, sleet, and ice. Eddie sat in the cockpit in the copilot's seat. Suddenly, they lost the radio beam. They began flying back and forth trying to find the radio beam, to no avail. They completely lost their bearings.

Eddie suggested that the pilot lower the plane below the clouds to get a view of the ground. The windows immediately iced over. Eddie opened his window and looked down. He could see treetops barely fifty feet beneath them. In a reflex, Eddie reached out his left hand and pulled the wheel back. The pilot pushed the throttle forward, and they went up.

More than a little nervous, Eddie tried to think calmly, clearly, and quickly. But before he had finished developing a plan, the radio went dead. The plane now was without range, radio, or any form of communication. They headed west, and after being up for seven hours, Eddie decided they should head down and have another look. The plane was running low on gas.

Down below, they saw a four-lane highway. "That road goes

from one place to another, or it wouldn't be there," Eddie said. The road went northwest, toward Chicago, so Eddie suggested they follow it.

Eddie glanced out his window to the right. By chance, he saw a flickering glow in the distance. It was a city. Eddie told the pilot to follow the light to the northeast. The city turned out to be Toledo, Ohio. They put the plane down in Toledo and refueled. When they filled the tanks, they learned that only seven or eight gallons had remained. That added up to only about ten minutes of flying. Also, both the beam antenna and the voice antenna had become encrusted with ice and snapped off, since they did not have a tension reliever or a spring. Eddie promptly made a report to the manufacturer with a recommendation. Within 30 days, all airplane antennas had a tension reliever. Once again, Eddie had narrowly escaped a disaster.

Then, in February 1941, Eddie survived the Atlanta crash (see chapter 1). Through this terrible experience, Eddie walked away with one benefit: He was reassured that his life was spared so that he could serve a good purpose. With the Japanese bombing of Pearl Harbor and the United States deep in another war, Eddie found his purpose. Upon request from General "Hap" Arnold, he left for Washington in the early part of March 1942.

Lost in
the Pacific

When Eddie arrived in Washington on that Monday morning in March, he met with Hap Arnold concerning his mission. Hap was concerned about the reports he had received regarding combat troops in training. The men did not have the "punch" that was required to perform the jobs they needed to do. Hap felt that Eddie would be an excellent candidate for a morale boost. With his past experience and reputation, Eddie's very breath would be the flame to ignite a fire beneath the men.

Eddie left immediately, along with General Frank O'D. "Monk" Hunter, a pilot who flew with Eddie in the 94th Squadron, and Colonel Hans Christian Adamson, a reservist who would be in charge of press relations. Hunter had recently recovered from a broken back, and he took a doctor with him. Not completely healed from the Atlanta crash, Eddie brought along a masseur. The group began visiting military bases throughout the United States.

Once on the road, Eddie found that he got along fine at the air bases by using a simple cane. When he stopped moving around, during flights between bases or when he relaxed at the end of the day, Eddie felt his muscles stiffen. At these times, the masseur would set to work, making Eddie limber again.

General Henry "Hap" Arnold enlisted Eddie's help in boosting the morale of pilots training for World War II. Eddie observed the pilots' enthusiasm, and concluded that the problem wasn't their morale, but a lack of excitement and action in their training.

During his visits at the air bases, Eddie met with pilots in training. He began his talks by insisting that he was not Captain or Colonel Rickenbacker, but plain Buck Private Rickenbacker. This introduction seemed to break the ice with the young men. He then shared with them stories about World War I, his combat experience and the type of planes he flew, and he talked about his experience with air-craft after the war. After discussing the Nieuport planes of World War I, and the little 30-caliber machine guns that would often jam, Eddie emphasized how lucky these pilots were to actually have something to fight with.

Before too long, Eddie discovered that the problem Hap spoke of was not with the pilots. These men were America's best—keen, inspired, and enthusiastic. Quite honestly, the men were bored. They craved some action. The air bases lacked the necessary equipment to give the pilots adequate hands-on training. More specifically, they needed planes.

Eddie made a report to Hap, suggesting that he supply each air base with enough equipment to properly train the pilots, and Hap quickly responded to Eddie's suggestion. In addition to the equipment, Eddie recommended that the "Hat-in-the-Ring" insignia be restored to the 94th Squadron. The insignia had been pulled prior to World War II.

Eddie made visits to air bases all across the United States, making notes and suggestions. In a letter to Eddie, Hap wrote, "Your recent epic trip throughout the entire length and breadth of the United States was an inspiration to us all. . . ."

Things went so well that Secretary of War Henry Stimson wanted to send Eddie on a worldwide mission. This time, Eddie would be inspecting U.S. air combat craft, both fighters and bombers, in all war arenas. He was to gather information comparing America's planes and the enemy's planes, all kept top secret until his return from abroad in early October.

The first leg of his tour would take him to England, Ireland, and Iceland. He spent fourteen days in England before heading to Ireland and Iceland; among his visits was a lunch with Prime Minister Winston Churchill. Eddie returned to Washington and made a confidential report to Mr. Stimson.

On October 19, 1942, Eddie boarded a Pan American Clipper bound for Hawaii. This time, Eddie was on a secret mission for the U.S. government, but he was to continue his tour of inspection as a cover for his "real" mission. Traveling with him once again was Colonel Hans Adamson. The plane landed in Honolulu the morning of October 20. After inspecting the air force units in Honolulu, Eddie planned to stop in Australia, New Guinea, and Guadalcanal. By evening of the 20th, Eddie was ready to leave. Commanding officer Brigadier General William L. Lynd promised to have a plane ready for Eddie by 10:30 that night.

Eddie hoped for a B-24 bomber, which was a roomy ship, but the only available aircraft was a Boeing Flying Fortress. The obsolete plane was marked for return to the United States for use in military training. General Lynd assured Eddie that the crewmen were all experienced members of the Army Air Transport Command. He would be flying in capable hands.

As they were packing the plane, Eddie learned an extra passenger would also be accompanying them: Sergeant Alexander Kaczmarczyk. Alex was a ground crew chief who had been hospitalized with a case of yellow jaundice. While he was recovering, he became ill with appendicitis. Still a little weak, but overall recovered, Alex was to rejoin his unit in Australia.

Eddie introduced himself to the pilot, Bill Cherry, a relaxed Texan. The copilot was Lieutenant James C. Whittaker.

The plane took off on time and was moving along at 80 miles per hour when a brake expander tube broke loose, partially locking one wheel. The plane lunged left. Eddie saw the dark shadows of the hangars getting closer. Cherry, with some clever maneuvering, managed to loop back onto the runway and avoid sending them plunging into the bay. After the plane stopped, Eddie told Cherry, "Mighty fine job. But I thought for a minute the tires never would hold."

Cherry laughed and responded, "You and me both."

Another plane was repaired, and they were rescheduled to take off at 1:30 in the morning. As the luggage and supplies were being transferred to the second plane, navigator John DeAngelis carefully examined his octant. Similar to a sextant, the octant was an instrument used in air and sea navigation to observe altitude and figure latitude and longitude. The octant had taken a hard hit during the take off, but it appeared to be unbroken.

Promptly at 1:30 A.M., they shot down the runway, this time making a successful liftoff. It was a beautiful night to fly. Scattered areas of thin clouds dotted the black sky, illuminated by a three-quarter moon. Eddie asked Cherry what the weather forecast was, to which Cherry responded that it would be an "uneventful flight." At five o'clock in the morning, Cherry decided to try to get some sleep, and Whittaker took over the controls. The instruments indicated that the plane had held a steady course all night. After a short while, Cherry came back. It was too cold at 10,000 feet to sleep.

While Whittaker was flying, Eddie came into the cockpit and asked how things were going. Whittaker said that all was well and asked if he'd like to take the controls.

Eddie smiled and said, "I've probably forgotten how to fly by instruments," but he took the controls for a while. Eddie and Cherry talked a while about the difference in planes between World War I and World War II. After their chat, Eddie left the cockpit to get some juice and a sweet roll. At about 8:30 A.M., Cherry descended below the clouds. They were scheduled to land at 9:30 A.M., and everything had gone as planned—until then, that is. Below the clouds, there was no land in sight. In every direction stretched the expansive blue waters of the Pacific.

The men decided that they could not have overshot the island, because they had kept careful track of their speed and tailwind. There was only one explanation—they had passed either northeast or southwest of the island. It was possible that the tailwind forecast was underestimated, or that the octant had been damaged to the point of inaccuracy. In any event, the same conclusion remained; they were lost and with only about four hours of fuel remaining.

Eddie asked Cherry what they were intending to do. Cherry told him they would first try the box procedure: fly in the shape of the box, all the while sending out signals to land, hoping someone would locate them or they would locate land. They would fly 45 minutes on each leg of the box. This would leave them with about an hour's fuel after they completed the box. Eddie stayed near the cockpit. He had been through desperate situations before and wanted to be nearby to offer whatever help he could. At the end of the last leg, the group was just where it had begun and without luck. They saw nothing. They heard nothing. And as far as they knew, no one had heard or seen them.

Cherry decided they would have to put the plane down on the ocean. It was a delicate procedure, but it could be done. However, as far as these men knew, no plane had ever been set down on the ocean without casualties. Many times, no one lived to tell about it.

A couple of risks existed. If the plane came down on a crest, the nose would plunge into the next wave and cave in. The plane probably would continue its downward dive. If the plane hit the crest too hard, it could break in two, the pieces disappearing immediately. Of course, every minute was of the essence, and there was sure to be some shock from the crash. That moment of shock could mean life or death.

After visiting bases in Hawaii, Eddie boarded a Boeing Flying Fortress that was to take him to the next leg of his tour in New Guinea. Navigational instruments failed, and the crew soon found themselves lost and running low on fuel. Eddie and seven crew members were forced to make a crash landing in the Pacific.

Realizing the situation, Eddie began to study his companions. The only man he knew was Hans, and although Hans may have been an adventurer in his youth, age had turned him, like Eddie, into an office man. The copilot, Lieutenant Whittaker, was a self-assured man about age 40. Navigator De Angelis was a wiry, thoughtful 23-year-old, recently married, and very perplexed at the malfunction of his instruments. Private Bartek was the flight engineer, age 20, serious, red-headed, and freckled. Bartek carried with him at all times a khaki-covered Bible, which would come in very handy in the days ahead. The radio operator was Sergeant James Reynolds, tall and thin, engaged, quiet, and competent. Then there was the extra passenger. Alex looked frail, not exactly ocean-bound material. Captain Cherry was a happy-go-lucky Texan, but Eddie remembered thinking, "My young friend, your cowboy boots and goatee are going to look pretty . . . funny in the middle of the Pacific."

The men put some food and water in a bag to take with them. Eddie stuffed his official papers from Mr. Stimson in his inside pocket, along with a chocolate bar. As Cherry brought the plane down, Eddie prepared the crew by shouting the distance to landing. "Twenty feet . . . ten feet . . . five feet . . . one foot, cut!" Cherry cut the engine. As the plane hit the water, there were cracks, bangs, and sounds of ripping metal. Eddie remembered the sounds—they were the same ones he heard during the Atlanta crash. Already water was filling up around Eddie's feet and falling down his back. A window had broken beside him, and Eddie looked out to what seemed like the entire Pacific heading in. Alex and De Angelis looked all right, but Hans was hurt, and Reynolds's face and hands were bleeding from contact with the radio equipment when they hit. But the plane was down, and everyone was still alive.

Without time to spare, they released the life rafts. One by one, they quickly exited the plane. What had looked like smooth glass from 5,000 feet was actually tossing and heaving waves 8 to 12 feet high. They had a lot of difficulty getting into the rafts. "So this," Eddie thought, "is the placid Pacific."

There were three rafts and eight men. DeAngelis and Alex took a doughnut raft. Cherry, Reynolds, and Whittaker took another raft, and Eddie, Bartek, and Hans took the third. Once in the rafts, the question was asked as to who had the food and water. In the confusion of the landing, no one had remembered to grab it. By this time, it was too late to go back into the plane. It would be going down in minutes. Anyone trapped inside would follow it to its watery grave. They found four oranges floating in the water and quickly gathered them up. The plane stayed afloat for almost six minutes. Then the tail tipped up, stood still for a moment, then slid down into the sea. It was 2:36 in the afternoon.

As the men lay in their rafts that first afternoon, they nervously watched the fins of sharks cut across the water. The sharks proved to be more a mental threat than a physical one. They would sometimes swim directly beneath the rafts, sliding their dorsal fins across the bottoms. Other than the nuisance of their constant companionship, the men did not get attacked by the sharks.

The first several days on the ocean were excruciating for the bunch. The days were scorching hot, and the nights chilled their flesh to the bone. Most of the men suffered severe sunburns. They had ditched most of their clothing before they got out of the plane. Eddie had kept his entire suit on, including his socks, shoes, and jacket. The clothing protected him from the sun, and somewhat from the cold sprays of water that continued to douse them all night long. The salt water added a mean element to their suffering as well, as it tends to eat away at the skin. Several of the men developed boil-like sores (salt water ulcers) from constantly sitting in salt water. The rafts themselves were incredibly inadequate. The larger rafts were barely large enough to hold one man, much less three, and the doughnut raft was even smaller. Later, Eddie reported these inadequacies to the military and recommended improvements to their size.

Eddie was in charge of rationing their only food, the oranges. He first cut them in half, then into quarters, and finally into eighths. This was their only nourishment for the first six days. Their hunger took over their every thought, and during the day, the men discussed all kinds of food, including the best restaurants. They often fantasized over chocolate malted milks.

On the eighth day, just as Eddie began to doze off, a gull appeared out of nowhere and landed right on his head. Everyone sat still and quiet. Eddie slowly reached his hand up toward his hat. He made no quick gestures, trying to sense the exact location of the gull's legs. When he thought he was near, Eddie closed his fingers hard. He had caught it. They proceeded to kill and defeather the bird, divided it up, and ate it raw. Eddie later remembered, "Even the bones were chewed and swallowed."

Eddie saved the intestines for fish bait. Reynolds had stashed some fishing line and a couple of hooks in his pocket before the plane went down. Eddie baited a hook and passed it over to Cherry. Pulling his ring off his finger, Whittaker handed it to Cherry to use as a weight. The line was barely in the water and a small mackerel took the bait. Eddie dropped the other line and quickly caught a sea bass. All this food in one day must have seemed like a feast to the starving men, and no one complained about eating it uncooked. The cool and wet fish meat even helped to quench their thirst. They ate one fish immediately and saved the other for the next day.

Another problem that continued to plague the men was the lack of fresh water. They could not drink the salt water—that would just dehydrate them. In fact, they had heard many stories about men lost at sea, parched from the intense heat, succumbing to temptation and drinking the salt water. The salt water would drive them mad with thirst, and Eddie continually reminded the men not to drink it, no matter how desperate they became. Their only water supply came from the occasional rain squalls. Since they did not know when the next rain would come, they tried to catch as much as they could, and saved it in the air compartments of their Mae Wests (life jackets).

Each night, they sent up a flare, hoping a plane or a ship

would see their distress signal. But each following day ended in disappointment. There seemed to be no sign of life for hundreds of miles around them. All the while, Bartek read from his Bible, and before long, the group joined together in daily prayer sessions. Prayer seemed to be their only hope at all, and the readings managed to help keep their spirits up. One of the passages they read every day was from the book of Matthew (Matthew 6:31–34). It read, "Therefore take no thought, saying, What shall we eat? Or, What shall we drink? . . . For your heavenly Father knoweth that ye have need of all these things. But seek ye first the kingdom of God, and his righteousness; and all these things shall be added unto you. . . . Take therefore no thought for the morrow: for the morrow shall take thought for the things of itself." A few of the men were not very religious before the crash, and at first were skeptical. But during the weeks on the Pacific, every man discovered some form of spirituality inside himself.

Alex had become very weak since the first day of the crash. His body hadn't fully recovered from the jaundice, and life on the open sea had taken a heavy toll on him. He was visited by fits of delirium, in which he babbled on about his mother and a girl. DeAngelis informed the others that he had been drinking sea water at night during his hallucinations. Eddie suggested that Alex switch places with Bartek and ride in his boat. During that night, Eddie cradled Alex like a child, trying to protect him from the cold ocean sprays. He gave him regular doses of water, and by morning he seemed better.

Alex moved back into the smaller raft with Bartek the following afternoon. But again that night, Alex worsened. At 2:00 in the morning, Bartek yelled to the others that he thought Alex was dead. Eddie and Cherry both confirmed Bartek's claim, but Eddie suggested they wait until morning to do anything. He did not want to make a tragic mistake about Alex's condition.

The dawn of the 13th morning came and Eddie once again examined Alex. The body was already stiffening, but he wanted to be absolutely positive before they committed the body to the sea. DeAngelis recited as much as he could remember of the Catholic burial service. They then zipped up Alex's flying suit, rolled him over the side of the raft, and watched him sink into the sea. This incident reminded the remaining seven of their own mortality, and they prayed even harder that they would soon be rescued.

On the 17th day, when all spirits were down and belief in a possible rescue was waning, a new surge of excitement and hope came to the men. A plane appeared out of a squall about five miles away. The men yelled and waved, trying to attract the attention of the pilot, but the plane flew by—not approaching any closer. Even with the frustration of not getting picked up, the men were overjoyed. This sign meant they were near some sort of civilization.

The next day they saw two more airplanes and waved their shirts in the air. Again, the planes flew past, not seeing the rafts. Captain Cherry decided he wanted to break away from the others. He felt if they separated, they would have a better chance of getting picked up. Eddie disagreed and tried to get him to stay with the group. But it was no use arguing— he had made up his mind. Not long after Cherry drifted out of sight, Whittaker and DeAngelis talked about breaking loose as well. Reynolds also was in their raft, too weak to move. Again, Eddie tried to discourage them, saying that Reynolds was too sick to understand what they were asking of him. But they insisted, and broke free.

Eddie was left in his raft with Hans and Bartek, both of whom were near comatose. He had about two quarts and a pint of water remaining, and he knew that in their emaciated condition they couldn't hold out much longer. On the 21st day, Bartek regained consciousness enough to alert Eddie of approaching planes. Eddie was too weak to stand, so from his

After 22 days at sea, Eddie and the remaining survivors were located and rescued. After a short recovery period, Eddie continued his mission, which was to relay a top secret message to General MacArthur in Australia.

seated position, he waved his old hat as vigorously as he could. The planes passed over only a few hundred yards off the water and only a couple of miles away, and then disappeared into the setting sun. Eddie believed this was their last chance and began to despair.

A half-hour later, Eddie heard the planes again. This time, they were coming closer. The first plane dived right over the raft. It came so close Eddie could see the pilot smiling and waving. Eddie noticed the insignia on the plane; it was the U.S. Navy, and he was filled with happiness and relief. All the while, Eddie continued to wave like a lunatic. He wanted to make sure the pilot knew they were still alive. The planes then disappeared for a short time.

Bartek kept asking, "Are they coming back? Are they coming back?"

"Yes, they know where we are, and they are certainly coming back," Eddie assured him.

The planes returned and began circling the raft. Eddie was not sure what the pilot's plan was. Night was fast approaching, and it looked like a storm was building to the south. The pilot then shot off a couple flares over the raft and it became clear to Eddie what he was doing. He was waiting for a boat.

The pilot made a careful landing on the water, which was for the most part smooth. Eddie paddled the raft up to the pontoon of the plane and grabbed hold. The radioman and the pilot helped pull Eddie close. The pilot then told Eddie that Cherry had been picked up about 25 miles away. The three men in Eddie's raft were the real lucky ones, though. During the night, their raft had drifted through a chain of islands and headed straight into open sea.

Over the previous 21 days, it was hard to estimate how far the men had drifted. Eddie figured it was somewhere between 400 and 500 miles. They had drifted across the International Date Line, so, according to their calendar, they were rescued on Wednesday, November 11; according to the pilot's, it was Thursday, November 12. They were a few hours into their 22nd day at sea.

The plane had room for only one passenger, so Eddie assumed that Hans, being the worst off, would be taken first, and he and Bartek would wait for the boat. Eddie asked if the plane could wait for the boat to arrive, so they wouldn't be missed in the dark. The pilot told Eddie that they would be coming along, too.

Eddie looked at the cockpit and asked, "Where?"

"On the wing," the pilot replied.

The pilot and radioman secured Eddie to left wing and Bartek to the right. The plane taxied along in the blackness, the propeller wash spraying Eddie's eyelids.

Once on the PT boat, Eddie was given water, blankets, and food. After sitting for so long, he found walking a very difficult task, and the rocking motion of the ocean made it difficult to stand up without falling over. The three men were taken to a nearby island. There they were reunited with Cherry and Whittaker, DeAngelis, and Reynolds, who also had been rescued. The men were immediately given medical treatment. The next afternoon, two doctors arrived from Samoa. They decided it was best to transfer all of the men to a better equipped hospital in Samoa, except Bartek and Reynolds, who were too sick to move.

On December 1, Eddie boarded a plane for Australia. He was determined to complete his secret mission and report back to General Arnold, which he did. In Australia, Eddie met with General Douglas MacArthur. He gave MacArthur the oral message that he was secretly carrying. He later made a full report to Stimson as well. Eddie later wrote, "Though I remember every word of it to this day, I shall not repeat it. Stimson and MacArthur took it with them to the grave, and so shall I."

Back at home, Eddie's family had never given up hope of his rescue. Adelaide was quoted by reporters as saying, "Eddie will turn up. He's too old to get lost in an airplane now." It was Adelaide's persistence that continued the search when the rest of America had written Eddie off. Newspaper articles around the country had assumed Eddie was dead. One editorial cartoon in the New York *Journal-American* ran the headline, "End of the Roaring Road?" The cartoon's creator was Burris Jenkins, Jr., a friend of Eddie's. After Eddie read the headline, he tore the cartoon out of the paper and wrote, "Hell, No!" across it and sent it back to Burris. The paper reprinted the cartoon with Eddie's commentary across it.

When the news spread of Eddie's rescue, newspapers hailed his survival record, assigning him names such as "Iron-man Eddie," "That Indestructible Man of Aviation," and "The Man Who Always Comes Back." Eddie was finally reunited with his family in Washington on December 19, 1942, at 9:00 in the morning. As Eddie came down the steps of the plane, he saw Adelaide, Dave, and Bill waiting for him. Bill broke through the group and ran to his father. Throwing his arms around him he cried, "Oh, Daddy, I'm so happy to see you again." Eddie was speechless.

The
Later Years

O ut of the suffering of eight men lost at sea came some crucial changes that benefited America and the world. First, ferrying operations in the South Pacific improved. And even before Eddie could turn in his recommendations to Stimson, many other improvements had already taken effect. Included in Eddie's recommendations were the importance of keeping proper logs and of making enhancements in radio and other forms of communication.

Naturally, an item of concern was the life rafts in which the men stayed for 22 days. Bill Cherry was ordered to Washington to help in redesigning rafts and survival equipment. First and foremost, the rafts were made wider and longer. Each raft was then supplied with a sheet of material that could be used as a sail, as protection against the sun, and as a rain catcher. A sealed, watertight box of emergency supplies and equipment accompanied every raft. Included in the box were liquids, concentrated food, vitamins, sedatives, knife, first-aid kit, rubber patches and waterproof glue, flares and pistols, and fishing tackle and bait.

The air force demonstrated the new rafts to Eddie. The raft Eddie reviewed was equipped with a radio and chemical

Eddie published the story of his days lost at sea first in *Life* magazine, and then as a book called *Seven Came Through*. He donated the profits to the Air Force Aid Society started by Hap Arnold and his wife.

water distillers that could desalinate the sea water at one and a half quarts a day. After inspecting the raft, Eddie affirmed that he could live for three months on a raft such as this and come back in good condition. The air force appropriately named the rafts "Rickenbackers."

After Eddie's incident on the Pacific, Hap Arnold and his wife decided to establish an Air Force Aid Society to help widows and children of airmen killed in action. Initially, Mrs. Arnold was not successful in raising much money. However, not long after Eddie's rescue, he began receiving offers from newspapers, magazines, and book publishers for his story of the Pacific ordeal. When he heard about the Air Force Aid Society, he decided to sell his story to the highest bidder and donate the money to the society. In New York, Eddie met with *Time* and *Life*. He accepted a bid from *Life* of $25,000. The story was set to run in three issues, becoming *Life's* first serial. The issue would also include a full-page ad devoted to the Air Force Aid Society.

Later, Doubleday & Company published *Seven Came Through*, Eddie's full-length account of the Pacific ordeal. Doubleday agreed to donate its profits to the Air Force Aid Society as well. Over the years, the book brought thousands of dollars to the organization, and its trustees insisted that Eddie become the president. Later, Eddie also became chairman of the National Policy Committee of the High School Victory Corps. In this position, Eddie traveled across the country speaking to young boys and girls, encouraging them to participate in the war effort by serving either in the armed forces or in the production lines. Feeling a closeness to American youth, Eddie took sincere enjoyment in inspiring America's young people.

Eddie received several suggestions that he run for political office, first as Ohio senator, then as president. When the ideas were proposed to Eddie on several occasions, he graciously declined the consideration. He believed he could better serve his country as a private citizen, who had an ear for the people, and that was the way he remained.

In Eddie's mind, the biggest change that the Pacific ordeal brought about was a spiritual one. Before those few weeks on the ocean, Eddie was quietly religious, admitting that "quite a few of his cronies" did not realize his spirituality. After the rescue, Eddie no longer had any shyness about expressing his true feelings. He believed that his rescue could be attributed to God's grace, and he wasn't ashamed to announce it. One columnist wrote: "Rickenbacker has become an evangelist without knowing it. . . ." But Eddie disagreed with one part of that statement—he knew it.

In early April 1943, Eddie went to see Secretary Stimson. He was ready to continue to serve as his special consultant if he so desired. Stimson gave Eddie an assignment that would take him around the world gathering vital military information. The assignment would take him from the West Indies to Natal, Brazil; across the Atlantic to Kakar, the westernmost point of Africa; up to Algiers, where General Eisenhower was directing the North Africa campaign; along the Mediterranean coast of Africa to Cairo, Egypt; and to Abadan and Tehran in Iran, which was the gateway to Russia. When Eddie realized his mission would bring him so close to the Russian door, he suggested that he be permitted to visit with the Russians as well. Stimson agreed that there was much to learn about the war in Russia and how the situation there affected the western front, but getting Eddie accepted by the Russian government would not be an easy task.

As it turned out, the U.S. government was not much help in getting Eddie into Russia. His only chance would be if President Roosevelt were to ask Premier Stalin personally, and since Eddie had publicly criticized Roosevelt's administration in its handling of the war, this did not seem a likely route. But Eddie had another idea. Secretly, he made plans with a governmental agency called Lend-Lease. This program sent American military supplies to nations fighting the Axis powers, including Russia. Eddie made arrangements with Lend-Lease to visit representatives in Russia. Once inside, he could have an eye on other operations as well. Eddie gave strict instructions that there was not to be a word to anyone regarding his plans to visit Russia.

Eddie went about his military business, finishing up in Tehran. At 6:00 on the morning of July 19, 1943, a C-87 took off headed toward Russia, with Eddie Rickenbacker passenger. When the plane landed in Moscow, Eddie was greeted by Russian officers and three Americans, one of whom was Admiral William H. Standley, the American ambassador in Russia, all looking very confused. They greeted Eddie and whispered, "What in the hell are you doing here, Eddie?" Eddie had enough time to whisper the reply—military secret. Later, when they were alone, Eddie fully explained the nature of his mission. Of course, Stimson soon learned about Eddie's arrival in Russia and once again agreed that his information about the Russian situation was too valuable to pass up. He allowed Eddie to stay.

A couple of days after arriving in Russia, Eddie had a luncheon with Foreign Minister Molotov and Marshal Georgi Zhukov. During the lunch, they asked Eddie what he wished to see on his visit. Eddie listed his requests and watched as the Russian interpreter carefully wrote them down. After Molotov and Zhukov heard the list they asked about Eddie's interpreter. Eddie explained that he did not have one and hoped they could supply him with an interpreter that was a good pilot, an aeronautical engineer, and who spoke English well enough that the two would be able to understand each other. This reply won the trust of the two men. They saw that Eddie's purpose in Russia was honest, and agreed to give him what he asked for.

The next day, Eddie reported to the Russian Air Force headquarters. There, he met with an old friend, Commander

Andrei Youmachev. In 1937, Eddie had entertained Andrei for a week in New York. The friendly reunion was another favorable stamp on Eddie's business in Moscow.

Even though Germans were bombing locations in Russia about 500 miles away, Eddie asked Andrei why the Germans had not attempted an attack on Moscow. Andrei smiled and handed Eddie a stopwatch. He told Eddie to push the button on the watch as soon as he telephoned orders. Eddie did just as Andrei instructed. In 39 seconds, one hundred American P-39s dotted the sky. There was Eddie's answer.

Strategically placed air bases surrounded Moscow in three concentric rings. Andrei took Eddie to one of the bases in the outside ring. At this base, Eddie saw a squadron of planes at the end of the runway, engines running and pilots at the controls. Each pilot served a four-hour tour of duty, ready to take off at an immediate order. The men then proceeded to a base within the second ring. At the second base, Eddie observed planes positioned at the end of the runway, pilots inside, but the engines were not running. The engines were started once an hour to keep them warmed up and prepared. Inside the third-ring base, pilots waited in a heated tent, planes just outside. The planes were warmed every two hours at this base.

"Commander," Eddie said, "now I understand thoroughly why the Germans do not attempt to bomb Moscow."

At each base, Eddie talked to the pilots, relaying his experience with the planes they were flying. He gave them tips on maneuverability and handling techniques. Pilots and engineers listened intently to Eddie's lectures, understanding that the Russian Air Force could greatly benefit from his technical information.

All the while, Eddie was 500 miles away from the ambitiously offensive Germans. It was June 1943, and the Germans did not show signs of giving up the offensive. It appeared as though the Germans had abandoned a frontal attack on

Moscow, and they were marching around to the south to come in the back way. Zhukov told Eddie that if they attack, the Russians will defend, and if they do not attack, the Russians will wait until winter and "tear them to sheds." Eddie was surprised at the frank statements Zhukov was speaking to him, and he later asked the Russian official why they were so open with him. "There are two kinds of foreigners whom we entertain," one of them said. "One kind is those we must, the other, those we like. You happen to fall in the latter category."

Eddie then was taken to visit the air regiments on the front. At his stops, Eddie spoke to pilots flying A-20s and P-39s. The P-39 pilots praised the American planes, noting that one of them had shot down a total of 27 Focke-Wulfs and Messerschmitts. Eddie learned that the Germans had decreased the number of planes on the Russian front from 2,700 to fewer than 2,000. Those planes had to go somewhere, and Eddie figured they must have gone to the western front.

The first night, Eddie awakened to violent shakes. He and the Russian officers hurried to nearby headquarters and went into the underground war room. The Germans had attacked. Eddie was standing in a room that had a large map of the entire front line on the wall. On the map, every major unit had been marked in universal military language. Eddie could hardly believe the information he had been exposed to. He calmly asked questions of General Antoshkin while he concentrated on the map, memorizing every detail.

Despite the beginning of a full German offensive in Russia, the Russians were content to let Eddie continue his mission there. The next day, Eddie made several visits, one of which was with Admiral Standley. Eddie gave him a careful report of what he had learned the previous night, along with a detailed description of the map. Standley wanted to send Eddie back to Washington with this information immediately. But Eddie argued that it would be suicide for him to leave now—after just receiving such classified information. Although America had become Allies with Russia against Germany, the Russians were still distrustful of Americans. For years, Americans had opposed Russia's actions. Eddie convinced the admiral it would be best for him to stay and complete his mission.

At the end of his visits, Eddie was convinced that the Red Army and the Red Air Force were growing stronger day by day. They had excellent military leadership. The groups were well disciplined and organized, comprising a capable military machine. Eddie returned to the United Kingdom and spoke with top British officers about the situation in Russia, including Mr. Churchill. Eddie then arrived back in the United States on August 7, 1943. Despite a cable urging President Roosevelt to meet with Eddie and discuss his visit in Russia, Eddie never spoke to the president about his findings. Roosevelt did not even respond to the cable, which to Eddie was statement enough.

Back at home, Eddie had catching up to do with Eastern Air Lines. The company was experiencing difficulties resulting from inefficiencies, equipment shortages, and personnel problems. Troubles of tightness continued through the war years, but after the war, employees began coming back. The number of employees increased from approximately 3,400 in 1944 to more than 6,700 in 1946. To account for the boom, Eddie began organizing a more complex management system to provide Eastern with a more stringent form of checks and balances. In the years following the war, Eastern maintained its position as the most prosperous operator in the entire airline industry.

On October 1, 1959, at age 70, Eddie decided that Eastern should have a younger chief executive. Malcolm A. MacIntyre took over as president and chief executive officer. Because MacIntyre had little experience in the airline industry, Eddie remained as director and chairman of the board. On December 31, 1963, Eddie finally retired from active management of Eastern. He was 73 years old.

Eddie managed Eastern Air Lines until he was 73 years old, overseeing innovations in both the technology of Eastern's aircrafts as well as in the company's management system.

Eight years before his retirement, Eddie had bought a 2,700-acre ranch in Texas. He thought it would be nice to have a place to retire to. But after a while there, the ranch did not hold as much appeal as it initially did. Adelaide was often lonely, and Dave and his wife, who lived with them, were ready to return to New York. Eddie made a surprising offer to the Alamo Area Council Boy Scouts of America, who were in search of a new summer camp. He donated a part of the ranch, including the house, the equipment, and the stock to the Boy Scouts. Adelaide and Eddie then bought a home in Miami, Florida, which they later sold when they returned to New York.

Even after World War II, Eddie continued to be active in the service of the United States. In one mission, former president Herbert Hoover asked Eddie to help form a task force to investigate intelligence services in the U.S. Army, Navy, Marine Corps, Air Force, and Central Intelligence Agency. He also spent a great deal of time speaking out against Socialist trends in the country. Eddie also made many predictions for the country's future, some of which came true, some of which did not. But one thing was certain—Eddie firmly believed in the push for advancement in technology, both in the air and on land.

In 1967, Eddie published his autobiography, *Rickenbacker*. It is a comprehensive and riveting story about a great life. In it, Eddie writes about his accomplishments with modesty and truth. He died in 1973, at age 83. Remembered most vividly as a famous aviator, Eddie's talents and achievements stretched far beyond those heights.

1890

October 8   Eddie born Edward Reichenbacher in Columbus, Ohio.

1904

August 26   Father William dies.

1904   Takes his first job at the Federal Glass Company.

1905   Takes his first automobile job at Evan's Garage.

1906   Begins working for Frayer-Miller Company.

September 22 Rides as a mechanic in his first race in New York.

1907   Leaves Frayer-Miller Company and goes to work for the Columbus Buggy Company as head of the experimental department.

1910   Races automobiles all over Nebraska and Iowa.

1912   Goes to work for Mason Company.

1913   Wins the Sioux City race.

1916

November   Takes his first plane ride.

1916–1917 Travels to Europe to race; suspected of being a German spy.

1917

April   Becomes a staff driver with the American Expeditionary Force in France.

1918

March   Is dispatched to the 94th Aero Pursuit Squadron (the Hat-in-the-Ring Squadron), the first all-American air unit to go into combat.

April 14   Becomes part of the first combat flight of the Hat-in-the-Ring Squadron.

April   Participates in his first air combat fight and takes his first victory.

May 30   Achieves his fifth victory, making him an American Ace.

September 24 Becomes commander of the Hat-in-the-Ring Squadron.

September 25 Leads an attack on no fewer than seven German aircraft of which he shot down two. This attack earned Eddie the Congressional Medal of Honor in 1930.

October 30	Achieves his 26th victory.
November 11	World War I ends, leaving Eddie the American Ace of Aces.
1919	Publishes *Fighting the Flying Circus*, a book about his World War I fighting experiences.
1920	Establishes the Rickenbacker Motor Company. (Serves as vice president until the company goes bankrupt in 1927.)
1922	
September 16	Marries Adelaide Frost, singer and ex-wife of racecar driver Russell Clifford Durant. (Cliff was the son of William Durant, the founder of General Motors, Chevrolet, and Durant Motors.) They were married in Greenwich, Connecticut.
1925	
January 4	David Edward Rickenbacker born.
1927	Purchases the Indianapolis speedway for $700,000.
1928	
March 16	William Frost Rickenbacker born.
1932	
April 29	Joins Aviation Corporation.
1932	Appointed vice president of North American Aviation.
1934	
February 19	Airmail contracts are cancelled with commercial airlines. Eddie cancels his commission as colonel in the Specialist Reserve in protest of the airmail situation.
1935	Becomes general manager of Eastern Air Lines.
1938	
January	Buys Eastern Air Lines, becomes both president and general manager of the airline.
1941	
February 26	Survives the Atlanta crash.
December 7	Japanese bomb Pearl Harbor. Eddie and Adelaide spend the rest of the day and night following the news on the radio.

1942

March	Travels to Washington, meets with General Hap Arnold about a mission for Eddie in World War II.
Summer	Inspects air force bases throughout the United States.
October 21	Survives a plane crash in the Pacific Ocean with seven other military servicemen.
November 12	After 22 days at sea, Eddie and six survivors are rescued from their life rafts.
1943	Publishes *Seven Came Through*, a book about the Pacific ordeal. The profits are donated to the Air Force Aid Society.
April	Accepts another mission. He secretly arranges a visit to Russia to learn more about their military position in the war.
August 7	Returns to the United States.
1947	Sells the Indianapolis Speedway.

1959

October 1	Retires as president of Eastern Air Lines.

1963

December 31	Completely retires from active management of Eastern Air Lines at age 73.
1967	Publishes his autobiography, *Rickenbacker*.
1972	Suffers a stroke, Adelaide worked with doctors and encouraged Eddie to recover.
1973	A few months after his stroke, Eddie accompanies Adelaide to Switzerland for treatment for her failing eyesight.
July 23 or 27	(conflicting sources) Dies of a heart attack in Zurich. He was 83 years old.

Adamson, Hans Christian. *Eddie Rickenbacker.* New York: Macmillan Company, 1946.

French, Joseph Lewis. *Aces of the Air.* Springfield, Mass.: McLoughlin Bros., Inc., 1930.

Kilduff, Peter. *Richthofen: Beyond the Legend of the Red Baron.* New York: John Wiley & Sons, Inc., 1993.

O,Connell, Robert L. *Fast Eddie.* New York: William Morrow and Company, Inc., 1999.

Rickenbacker, Edward V. *Fighting the Flying Circus: Wings of War.* New York: Frederick A. Stokes Company, 1919.

——. *Rickenbacker.* Englewood Cliffs, N.J.: Prentice-Hall, Inc., 1967.

——. *Seven Came Through: Rickenbacker's Full Story.* Garden City, N.Y.: Doubleday, Doran and Company, Inc., 1943.

William F. Rickenbacker, ed. *From Father to Son: The letters of Captain Eddie Rickenbacker.* New York: Walker and Company, 1970.

Swarthout, Lind. *Captain Eddie Rickenbacker: God Still Answers Prayers.*

Thayer, Lucien H. *America's First Eagles.*

Whittaker, Lieutenant James C. *We Thought We Heard the Angels Sing.* New York: E. P. Dutton & Company, Inc., 1948.

FURTHER READING

Rickenbacker, Edward V. *Fighting the Flying Circus: Wings of War.* New York: Frederick A. Stokes Company, 1919.

——. *Rickenbacker.* Englewood Cliffs, N.J.: Prentice-Hall, Inc., 1967.

——. *Seven Came Through: Rickenbacker's Full Story.* Garden City, N.Y.: Doubleday, Doran and Company, Inc., 1943.

Whittaker, Lieutenant James C. *We Thought We Heard the Angels Sing.* New York: E. P. Dutton & Company, Inc., 1948.

Rachel A. Koestler-Grack has worked with non-fiction books as an editor and writer since 1999. During her career, she has worked extensively with historical topics, ranging from the colonial era to the civil rights movement. In addition, she has authored numerous historical biographies. Rachel lives with her husband and daughter on a farm near Glencoe, Minnesota.

PICTURE CREDITS